THE AUTHORITY O

G000145011

EXPLORING
FAITH
Theology for Life

SERIES EDITORS: Leslie J Francis and Jeff Astley

THE AUTHORITY OF THE BIBLE

William Strange

DARTON·LONGMAN + TODD

First published in 2000 by
Darton, Longman and Todd Ltd
1 Spencer Court
140-142 Wandsworth High Street
London SW18 4JJ

ISBN 0-232-52370-3

A catalogue record for this book is available from the British Library.

Designed by Sandie Boccacci
Phototypeset in Minion by Intype London Ltd
Printed and bound in Great Britain by
Page Bros, Norwich, Norfolk

CONTENTS

PREFACE

At the beginning of the third millennium a new mood is sweeping through the Christian Churches. This mood is reflected in a more radical commitment to discipleship among a laity who wish to be theologically informed and fully equipped for Christian ministry in the secular world.

Exploring Faith: theology for life is designed for people who want to take Christian theology seriously. Taken seriously, Christian theology engages the mind, involves the heart, and seeks active expression in the way we live. Those who explore their faith in this way are beginning to shape a theology for life.

Exploring Faith: theology for life is rooted in the individual experience of the world and in the ways through which God is made known in the world. Such experience is related to and interpreted in the light of the Christian tradition. Each volume in the series takes a key aspect of theology, and explores this aspect in dialogue with the readers' own experience. Each volume is written by a scholar who has clear authority in the area of theology discussed and who takes seriously the ways in which busy adults learn.

The volumes are suitable for all those who wish to learn more about the Christian faith and ministry, including those who have already taken Christian basic courses (such as *Alpha* and *Emmaus*) and have been inspired to undertake further study, those preparing to take theology as an undergraduate course, and those already engaged on degree programmes. The volumes have been developed for individuals to work on alone or for groups to study together.

Already groups of Christians are using the *Exploring Faith: theology for life* series throughout the United Kingdom, linked by an exciting initiative pioneered jointly by the Anglican dioceses, the Board of Education of the Church and World Division and the Ministry Division of the Archbishops' Council of the Church of England, the National

Society and the Church Colleges. Used in this way each volume can earn credits towards one of the Church Colleges' Certificates and provide access to degree level study. Further information about the Church Colleges' Certificate Programme is provided on page 119.

The Church Colleges' Certificate Programme integrates well with the lifelong learning agenda which now plays such a crucial role in educational priorities. Learning Christians can find their way into degree-bearing programmes through this series *Exploring Faith: theology for life* linked with the Church Colleges' Certificates.

This series of books originated in materials developed by and for the Aston Training Scheme. Thanks are due to former staff of the Scheme, and in particular to Roger Spiller who conceived of and commissioned the original series, and to Nicola Slee who edited the original materials. In the light of the closure of Aston, this series represents something of the ongoing contribution of the Scheme to the life of the Church.

In preparing a series of this kind, much work is done behind the scenes. Financial and staff support have been generously given by the Ministry Division. Thanks are due to Marilyn Parry for the vision of bringing together the Aston materials and the Anglican Church Colleges of Higher Education. We are also grateful for financial support from the following Church Colleges: Chester College; Christchurch University College, Canterbury; The College of St Mark & St John, Plymouth, St Martin's College, Lancaster; Trinity College Carmarthen; and Whitelands College (Roehampton Institute). Without the industry, patience, perception, commitment and skill of Ruth Ackroyd this series would have remained but a dream.

The series editors wish to express their personal thanks to colleagues who have helped them shape the series identity, especially Diane Drayson, Evelyn Jackson and Katie Worrall, and to the individual authors who have produced high quality text on schedule and so generously accepted firm editorial direction. The editorial work has been supported by the North of England Institute for Christian Education and the Centre for Ministry Studies at the University of Wales, Bangor.

Leslie J Francis
Jeff Astley

INTRODUCTION

The aim of this book is to help the reader to think about the Bible as Christian Scripture. It will not be addressing directly the problems of biblical interpretation: those are dealt with in a companion volume in this series (Evans, 1999). The focus of this present book is on the nature of the Bible as Scripture and on its authority for the Christian and for the Church. Biblical interpretation is, of course, very closely bound up with questions about the Bible's authority (Goldingay, 1995, p. 3; Bauckham, 1999, p. 20). How we interpret the Bible and what we think of the nature of the Bible are two sides of the same coin, but it is still legitimate for us to examine the Bible in itself and ask what is the place of this collection of books in the life of the Church and what should it be.

For anyone who reads the Bible as Christian Scripture these issues are almost bound to be matters of deep personal concern. We will be giving a lot of attention to the ways in which biblical criticism has altered our understanding of the Bible. Some readers may come to this topic already convinced that biblical criticism is a good thing, and that an unthinking fundamentalism is in danger of making the Bible seem incredible to modern people. Others may be passionately convinced of the opposite view, that many theologians and Church leaders are disregarding the truth of Scripture in order to compromise with unbelief. Others again may be uncertain how to explain what the Bible means for them and why it plays such a large part in the Church's life.

This book is meant to help people in any of these positions to work out more clearly what they can believe about the Bible. It is certainly not intended to undermine anyone's sincerely held beliefs about the Bible. It will ask questions about the Bible and it will invite you as the reader to think critically about a variety of beliefs concerning the Bible. The book will have done its job, not if it makes you change your views, but if it enables you to clarify and explain what you believe about the Bible, and why.

The New Revised Standard Version of the Bible is used for quotations.

1. THE BIBLE AND THE WORD OF GOD

Introduction

In this chapter, our task will be to get our bearings for the chapters to follow. We will examine Christian Scripture in three dimensions: *first*, the dimension of its quality or properties (does it have an inherent property which marks it out from all other literature?); *second*, the dimension of function (does it address us as the voice of God from 'outside', or is it a voice from 'within', the witness of past believers to their faith?); *third*, we shall examine the method to be used in coming to a conclusion about the Bible (do we first try to arrive at a theological understanding of Scripture, and then fit in the observable facts about it, or do we build up a theological picture from our analysis of, for instance, the Bible's historical reliability?).

Reflecting on experience

The following statements are meant to help you begin to reflect on what you think about the Bible. For each one, choose one response ranging from agree strongly to disagree strongly. Keep a note of your responses: we will come back to the same set of statements at the close of this book, to see whether you consider that your understanding has been clarified by what you have read and by the ideas you have thought about.

	Agree strongly	Agree	Neither agree nor disagree	Disagree	Disagree strongly
1. The Bible is inspired by God	AS	A	N	D	DS
2. God speaks to people through the words of the Bible	AS	A	N	D	DS
3. Modern scholars have weakened people's confidence in the Bible	AS	A	N	D	DS
4. There are no errors in the Bible	AS	A	N	D	DS
5. Science makes the Bible hard to accept	AS	A	N	D	DS
6. The Old Testament sometimes contradicts the New	AS	A	N	D	DS
7. Readings from the Apocrypha should not be included in Christian worship	AS	A	N	D	DS
8. Christians ought to believe what the Bible says	AS	A	N	D	DS

The authority of the Bible

How does the Bible relate to the Church and to the individual? Before we can decide what answer we will give to that question, we have to consider a wide range of evidence which we will look at in the next eight chapters, after which we will attempt to draw the threads together in chapter ten. In particular, we will need to think about the following areas.

- What is 'inspiration' and what part should Christians believe that God played in the production of the Bible?
- What does the scholarly investigation of the Bible tell us about its nature?
- How do we link the Bible with other sources of understanding about the world, such as science and history?
- How did the Church come to recognise which books were part of its Old and New Testaments?
- How do Christians integrate the Old Testament with the New?

EXERCISE
📖 **Read Luke 4:14–30.**

The Bible itself contains very little reflection on its own nature and purpose. But stories such as this one, Luke's narrative of Jesus' sermon at Nazareth, bring out some aspects of what Jews of the New Testament era perceived their Scriptures to be, and give an idea of how the early Christians also understood their Scriptures.

- In what setting were the Scriptures read (v. 16)?
- Does this story give any sense of connection between Old Testament and New (v. 21)?
- The congregation became angry (v. 28), presumably because they did not like what they were hearing about scriptural examples of God bringing healing or salvation to Gentiles (vv. 25–27). Does this depth of feeling about the interpretation of Scripture suggest anything about the respect which was accorded to Scripture, and of its importance?

The properties of Scripture: the objective-subjective dimension

The Bible is marked out from all other books in a variety of ways. Some editions of the Bible will have the words 'Holy Bible' on the cover, expressing a widespread sense among Christians (and Jews, as far as the Hebrew Scriptures are concerned), that there is something special which sets this book apart and makes it 'holy'. When we open a Bible, we are quite likely to find the special nature of this book indicated by the layout of each page: few, if any, other books are printed in two narrow columns. Although some modern versions are trying to break with this age-old tradition, the conventional layout of the Bible gives its special status a visual expression. In a Christian or Jewish act of worship, it is the Bible which we expect to hear read, just as the congregation in Capernaum in the time of Jesus gathered to hear their Scriptures read and preached upon.

The Bible as cultural icon

What is it which makes the Bible special? One answer might be that it is the Bible's status as an indispensible part of our cultural fabric. In the long-running British radio programme 'Desert Island Discs', celebrities are invited to choose eight records which they would want to take with them if they were to be 'cast away alone on a desert island'. With their records they can take one book, but on the assumption that they already have two books on their island: the Bible and Shakespeare. On this view, the significance of the Bible is parallel to that of Shakespeare – it has had a formative influence over many centuries on our culture, and especially on the culture of the English-speaking world through the majestic 1611 translation known in Britain as the Authorised Version (AV) and elsewhere as the King James Version (KJV).

But this cannot be the root of the Bible's significance. It would not have been treasured by generations of writers and artists, nor would it have been the inspiration of millions of otherwise unkown people, if these people had not believed that it had an intrinsic importance. Bunyan would not have drawn on the Scriptures for the imagery of *Pilgrim's Progress* if he had simply thought that the Bible was a kind of cultural icon. The Bible made an impact on our culture because the people who moulded that culture believed that the Bible had the authority to shape their world-view.

The Bible as word of God

We come back to our question: what makes the Bible special? Many Christians would say that it is important because it is the word of God (although nowhere in the Bible itself is Scripture ever referred to by this term). What is intended by describing Scripture as the word of God is: (a) that as a matter of history God was responsible for inspiring the books which make up our Bible; and (b) that as a matter of present experience God speaks through these words today. James Packer gives a particularly lucid expression of this view:

> The scriptural approach to Scripture is thus to regard it as God's written testimony to Himself. When we call the Bible the Word of God, we mean, or should mean, that its message constitutes a single utterance of which God is the author. What Scripture says, He says. When we hear or read Scripture, that which impinges on our mind (whether we realize it or not) is the speech of God Himself. (Packer, 1958, p. 89)

The Bible as a fact of Christian tradition

James Barr has offered another way of understanding the place of Scripture. In a lecture given in 1979, he asked the question: 'Why this book, or rather collection of books, and not some other? Does it just happen accidentally to be the Bible that is authoritative, or is there some *reason* for the centrality which we have been ascribing to it?' His answer was, partly, that the biblical books are the only authentic tradition from historic Israel and the only information about Jesus to have survived from first-century Christians. But he also argued that the biblical books had arisen out of the *tradition*, first of Israel, then of the Church. It arose out of the ongoing experience of the community of faith, and that experience carries on. The experience of people in the biblical period was not in essence different from that of the postbiblical community, but first Jews and then Christians decided to accept this segment of their story as authoritative, as Scripture:

> Thus in a way if one asks why the Bible should be taken as authoritative in relation to the later growth and development of Christianity, the answer is that that decision was in fact taken long ago and has thus long been built into the structure of Christianity. The acceptance of Scripture as something different in function from other tradition has been made by that other tradition itself. (Barr, 1980, p. 59)

A similar argument had been developed in the Roman Catholic context by Karl Rahner (see McGrath, 1995, pp. 72–75).

EXERCISE
The previous section has introduced us to two different approaches to the distinctiveness of the Scriptures. One view maintains that there is a quality inherent in the Scriptures (they are the ▶▶

word of God), the other that they are human writings to which the community of faith has ascribed an important status. Which do you consider is the more helpful way of understanding the distinctiveness of the Scriptures?

The function of Scripture: a word from outside or from within?

One traditional way of understanding the Bible has been to take the prophetic experience as a model. As God inspired prophets with a message, so to speak from 'outside', so all biblical writers received a message from God to pass on to their readers and hearers. On this view the whole of Scripture is a kind of prophecy, or oracle, through which God speaks.

This is a very ancient understanding of Scripture. The early Christians inherited from their Jewish background the belief that the prophets were inspired by the Holy Spirit, and that this inspiration extended even to those, such as David, who were not strictly 'prophets' (see, for example, Matthew 22:43 and Acts 1:16). In the second century a Christian writer named Athenagoras explained to those whom he wished to convince of the truth of the Christian faith that the prophets of the Old Testament had been passive recipients of a message from God, and to do so he used a striking image: the prophets 'lifted in ecstasy above the natural operations of their minds by the impulses of the Divine Spirit, uttered the things with which they were inspired, the Spirit making use of them as a flute-player breathes into a flute' (Athenagoras, *Plea for the Christians*, 9: on the internet at http://www.ccel.org/fathers2/).

EXERCISE
📖 **Read 2 Peter 1:19–21.**

In this passage, the 'prophetic message' (v. 19), which some translations take as 'the message of the prophets' (NEB), probably refers to the whole Old Testament, which the author takes as a complex of messianic prophecy. What would you say that this passage is affirming about the origin of the Old Testament Scriptures?

When we turn to look at the Bible itself, we soon find that not all the writing in it will really fit this prophetic model. There are places at which writers make clear that they were not receiving a message 'from outside', but gathering information from quite mundane sources, such as archives (Ezra 7:11–26) or eyewitness accounts and written narratives (Luke 1:1–2), or even their own memories, which could let them down at times (1 Corinthians 1:16)!

Later in this book we will examine something of the implications of modern scholarly study of the Bible. One such implication has been a clear focus on the humanity of the authors of Scripture. When we start to differentiate between various parts of the Bible, we find that the human authors and their communities influenced what was said: the concerns and language of an Amos are not the same as those of an Ezekiel, and Matthew presents Jesus in a distinctively different way from John.

Many interpreters today would argue that we should begin our understanding of Scripture, not by seeing it as a message coming direct from God, but as the product of human reflection and response to God (as people conceived him) first in Israel and then in the Church. Such a view of Scripture as genuinely *human* writings does not necessarily rule out divine activity in the production of the Scriptures. This view, though, asks us to read the Scriptures first as the writings of human beings in their own particular religious and cultural situations, and only when we have done that to go on (if we will) and read them as documents of faith.

This second view enables us to accommodate a number of features of the biblical writings which might seem difficult to reconcile with direct divine dictation. It takes into account failings of knowledge or of spiritual and ethical insight in the biblical writings (the assumption of a three-decker universe, or the presence of the vindictive Psalms, for instance). It allows us to appreciate development and change over time in the biblical writers' understanding of God and the world. It enables us to say that the books of the Bible show us how other people understood and approached the God whom we also worship. On this view, the Bible can be seen not so much as a message *from* God *to* humans, but as a series of messages *from* humans *to* their fellow human beings *about* God.

EXERCISE

It is usual in many churches for the reader to conclude a biblical reading with the sentence, 'This is the word of the Lord', to which the congregation responds, 'Thanks be to God.'

Do you think that there could be passages of the Bible for which that response might be inapproprate? You could consider the following passages:

- 1 Chronicles 8: In what sense does this have a message from God for us today?
- Psalm 88: Is this God addressing us, or a particularly mournful worshipper addressing God, who seems to have forgotten him?

Do you think that Christians should attend to *all* the Scripture as at least potentially having a word or message for the people of God (2 Timothy 3:16)?

Method: theoretical or empirical?

There are two ways in which we can arrive at a view of what the Bible is as Christian Scripture.

One way, the theoretical, starts by forming a theoretical framework of understanding – arriving first at a theological decision on what the Bible must be. It only then looks at the details of its contents and history to see how these match the theory.

The other way, the empirical, starts by observation of what the Bible is – when, how and by whom it was written, how the ideas in it relate together, and so on. This approach constructs its view of Scripture only when it has tried to form a considered opinion on what have been called the 'phenomena' of Scripture – the details of its contents and what can be known of its history and development.

The theoretical method

The first way of arriving at a view of the Bible as Christian Scripture does not necessarily entail accepting the 'prophetic' model which was described in the previous section, but this method is commonly used by writers who espouse that view of Scripture. A classic instance would be the nineteenth-century Protestant B B Warfield, who began his account of the nature of the Bible by examining Scripture's attestation to itself. From texts such as 2 Timothy 3:16, 2 Peter 1:19–21 and John 10:34–36, Warfield argued that the Bible itself teaches that it is inspired by God in every part, true in everything it states, and can never be set aside.

Warfield's view has been enormously influential in modern evangelical Christianity, as we shall see. But this type of theoretical approach is open to criticism on the grounds that the facts may not fit the theory: for instance, that there may be inconsistencies in the Bible, or that it conflicts with things we can demonstrate to be true from our scientific knowledge. Warfield himself gave surprisingly little attention to these criticisms. This was because, as he explained, if you have arrived on good evidence (as he believed he had) at a particular proposition (in this case the inerrancy of Scripture), then as long as the evidence which led you to the proposition remains unrefuted, all 'so-called objections' become merely 'difficulties' which must be adjusted to the proposition (Warfield, 1948, p. 174). Warfield's 'theoretical' method has been explained in this way:

> To put it another way, the doctrine of inspiration [in Warfield's thought] is a vast hypothesis functioning methodologically like the Copernican theory or the theory of evolution. Anyone who relies on the hypothesis has the confidence that any conflicts that appear between facts and the hypothesis can be explained within the framework of the hypothesis. It would take an enormous number of conflicts to raise serious doubts about the hypothesis. (Kelsey, 1975, p. 22)

The empirical method

An alternative approach to the Bible will be found in many books and articles which favour an empirical method. In this approach to the Bible, priority is given to what we can discern the biblical books to be, and a theory about the nature of the Bible will only be constructed from those observations. What Warfield referred to as 'difficulties' might prove in fact (on this view) to be vital clues to understanding the true nature of the biblical writings.

To take one example: in Matthew 21:4–7 we are told that Jesus rode into Jerusalem on an ass and a colt, but in Mark 11:7 on a colt alone. On Warfield's view it is necessary to harmonise the two accounts, and propose that there were two animals but that Mark chose only to mention one. Warfield's proposition (inerrancy) can thus survive what might seem an objection to it. The empirical approach, though, would not oblige us to bring the accounts into harmony, but would ask what *reason* each evangelist might have for describing the scene differently. It might lead us to conclude that Matthew interpreted the text of Zechariah rather literally ('your king . . . mounted on an ass, and on a colt'), and invented the extra animal to make the story conform to the prophecy. The method *need* not lead us to that conclusion, but it is open to do so. Instead of deciding beforehand that the scriptural passages must both be literal historical accounts, this empirical approach would first enquire what is the most likely explanation of the facts, and then go on to deduce what sort of literature these biblical books must be.

The approach has been described succinctly by John Barton:

> Much Christian thinking about the Bible typically proceeds by trying to make basic assumptions about what the Bible 'must' be like. We imagine what kind of book we would give to the human race if we were God, and wanted to communicate the truth about ourselves. . . . But I believe one should begin, not from hypothetical ideas about what kind of book God can be supposed to want us to have, but from the observable character of the Bible we have actually got. If it is indeed a divine intention that gave us this book . . . God must have wished us to have, not a neat set of definitions, but a large and varied range of books, written at many different times and forming a unified corpus only as the end product of a lengthy process of selection and reception. (Barton, 1997a, pp. 39–40)

EXERCISE

Here are two questions to think over on the subject of each of the two approaches to the Bible we have been considering.

- What kind of evidence do you think would be sufficient to provide a refutation of Warfield's view that the Bible is inerrant?
- Is the empirical approach as open-ended as it seems? Is such a critical approach ever able to discern Scripture as the word of God, or will it inevitably conclude (because of the kind of questions it asks) that biblical books are human literature much like any other?

Further reading

Barr, J (1980), *Explorations in Theology* 7, London, SCM.

Barton, J (1997), *What is the Bible?* London, SPCK (second edition).

Bauckham, R (1999), *Scripture and Authority Today*, Cambridge, Grove.

Evans, R (1999), *Using the Bible: studying the text*, London, Darton, Longman and Todd.

Goldingay, J (1995), *Models for Interpretation of Scripture*, Grand Rapids, Michigan, Eerdmans and Carlisle, Paternoster.

Kelsey, D H (1975), *The Uses of Scripture in Recent Theology*, London, SCM.

McGrath, A E (ed.) (1995), *The Christian Theology Reader*, Oxford, Blackwell.

Packer, J I (1958), *'Fundamentalism' and the Word of God*, London, IVP.

Warfield, B B (1948), *The Inspiration and Authority of the Bible*, Phillipsburg, New Jersey, Presbyterian and Reformed Publishing.

2. SCHOLARS AND THE SCRIPTURES

Introduction

If you picked up a few books on the Bible in any bookshop today, you would be likely to find that they fell into two categories. In one category would be those books written for people who want to read the Bible from a perspective of faith. These would probably treat the Bible as a fairly straightforward factual account of things as they happened. They would also be concerned to explain what the text means for us today. In the other category would be those books written from a scholarly perspective. These would tend to argue, or even assume, that things did not invariably happen just as the biblical narratives relate. Their interest would be in what the text meant when originally written, no matter how strange or irrelevant to us its orginal meaning might appear.

There are, of course, scholarly books which are also supportive of conventional faith, and there are devotional books which accept the way in which scholars criticise the Bible. But the two approaches to the Bible mentioned above probably describe a large number of the books you would find on the shelves today.

To whom, then, does the Bible really belong: the scholar or the believer? How has it come about that there are such different ways of reading the Bible? Is one right and the other wrong? Is there a way of bringing these two kinds of Bible reading together?

> ### Reflecting on experience
> How do you deal with a passage of Scripture which is difficult to accept as it stands, or which is in tension with some other passage?

Let us take an example:

EXERCISE

📖 **Read Matthew 20:29–30 and Mark 10:46–47.**

How would you explain these parallel passages? Would you try to find a way of making them both factually accurate (for example there were two men, but Mark concentrates on one)? Or would you say that one gospel writer has got his facts mixed up (for example Matthew wanted to make the miracle bigger by adding a second blind man)?

Think about your own reasons for favouring one way rather than another of solving the problem – why have you taken your own particular way of dealing with it? How important is it to reconcile different accounts of the same event?

Early criticism

It is no new thing that scholars and 'ordinary believers' should read and understand the Scriptures in different ways. As far back as the third century this gap can already be observed.

Origen (c. 185–254), a distinguished Christian scholar from Alexandria in Egypt, thought that it was legitimate and even necessary that the scholar should understand the Scriptures differently from what we might call the 'lay' Christian, or what Origen himself called the 'simple believers'. These simple believers read the Scriptures literally and superficially, and so did not notice the difficulties which careful scrutiny of the text threw up. Some of the difficulties were moral: how could the punishment of the wicked really be 'eternal' (Matthew 18:8) if, as Origen assumed, God's punishment is meant to reform the sinner? Some of these difficulties were historical: Mark, Luke and John say that Jesus rode into Jerusalem on one donkey, but Matthew says on two. They cannot all be right in point of historical fact.

The 'simple believer' accepted the doctrine of eternal punishment without trying to relate it to a philosophical system, and read the four gospels without worrying if the details did not tie up. But these things worried Origen, not least because they gave ammunition to critics of Chistianity who claimed that the Christians' Bible said unworthy things about God and contained contradictions. It also worried him that an uncritical reading of the Scriptures led the simple believers to believe such things about God as he considered would not be believed even by 'the most savage and unjust of men'.

Origen's answer was *allegory*. Non-Christian Greek scholars had already used this method to explain some of the less acceptable features of traditional legends about the gods. Origen applied the same method to scriptural writings and looked for a *spiritual* meaning in the text. He was convinced that the purpose of Scripture was to support faith, not to give information about the past. So, Origen argued, we should not worry if there are things in the Scriptures which seem unlikely or even impossible – for instance, how could there have been 'evening and morning' in the creation story before the sun had been created? For Origen, even things in the Bible which could not be accepted as literal and historical statements could be interpreted as allegories in a spiritual sense.

To take one example of how Origen set about this spiritual interpretation: Matthew 21:1–7 states that Jesus entered into Jerusalem on 'a donkey, and on a colt, the foal of a donkey'. Origen argued that for such a short journey only one animal would have been needed, so the three gospel writers who tell us that Jesus rode on one donkey were literally correct. But Matthew had been inspired by God to write of two animals, so the Holy Spirit has a message here, if we can find it. The Spirit is inviting us to disregard this as a literal account (which we see it cannot be) and to explore it as a spiritual account, an allegory. Origen suggests that since there was an older and a younger animal they represent the Old and the New Testament. The older beast was untied by the disciples of Jesus, representing the explanation of the Old Testament by the apostles. This donkey was also a beast of burden, representing the burdens or difficulties which the Old Testament presents. The way in which the two animals carried Jesus into the city symbolises the way in which the Bible, Old and New Testament together, brings Christ into the soul of the believer (*Commentary on John* 10.18.172–216, text available on the internet at http://www.newadvent.org/fathers).

EXERCISE
Origen thought that a biblical writer could be *factually* wrong but *spiritually* right, as Matthew was over the entry of Jesus into Jerusalem. Origen raises the question of 'truth' which we will examine in a later chapter, but he also raises the question ▶▶

of whether we as readers and critics *should* be able to say that a passage of Scripture is 'wrong' in some sense.

Consider whether it is necessary to accept the following passages in a literal sense, or to exercise some sort of criticism on them:
• the creation story (Genesis 1:1 to 2:4);
• the sun standing still for Joshua (Joshua 10:12–14);
• Jesus transfigured in the presence of the disciples (Matthew 17:1–8).

Modern criticism

A divide was already opening up in Origen's time between the 'simple believers' and scholars such as Origen who noticed problems which others did not see, and proposed solutions which others would not accept. That divide became more pronounced in the nineteenth century with the development of modern criticism.

In a later chapter we will come to look at the way in which science began to raise questions about the Bible and its statements. However, even before the scientific questioning of the Bible in the later nineteenth century, scholars were opening the Bible to scrutiny in a way which many Christians found shocking and destructive. The modern gap between the academic and the devotional reading of Scripture, which we noted at the start of this chapter, was opening up. How did this gap come into being, and is it inevitable?

The growth of modern criticism of the Bible can be linked to the movement of thought in the eighteenth century known as the *Enlightenment*, which changed the way in which western people looked at themselves, at the world, and at God (Reventlow, 1984; Rogerson, 1984; O'Neill, 1991). In particular, we can identify three new ways of looking at the Bible which characterised modern, post-Enlightenment biblical criticism.

Religion does not depend on history
Traditionally, Christians have supposed that their faith is 'historical', in the sense that certain things happened in history which have altered the relationship of God with humanity, such as the Exodus of Israel, or the resurrection of Jesus. The Bible is the divinely ordained record of these foundational facts.

During the eighteenth century several thinkers began to question whether religion does or even can rest on historical facts in this way. A faith which depends on stories of miracles is vulnerable, since we have no proof that these miracles ever took place. Surely, it was further argued, the truth about God should also be something accessible to everybody at all times, not the privilege of a few who have received a special revelation. And anyway, how can the truths of religion (which must be eternal, 'necessary' truths, such as God's love) be *made* true by something which happened in history?

This last point was made most strongly by a German thinker, Gotthold Ephraim Lessing (1729–1781), in a study published in 1777. He pointed out that Origen could appeal to miracles as evidence for the truth of Christianity, but miracles no longer happened in the eighteenth century, so there is no point in appealing to them in the contemporary world. Mere historical reports are not enough to establish that a particular event (such as a miracle or a resurrection) has taken place. And even if these events did take place, we cannot jump from making a *historical* statement such as 'Christ raised a dead man to life' to making a *theological* statement, such as 'God has a Son who is of the same essence as himself', on the basis of that historical 'fact'. This is Lessing's statement of the weakness of history as a basis for religion: 'If no historical truth can be demonstrated, then nothing can be demonstrated by means of historical truths. That is: the accidental truths of history can never become the proof of the necessary truths of reason' (Lessing, 'On the Proof of Spirit and Power', in McGrath, 1995, p. 154).

Lessing was very influential on the generations that followed. If one accepts his argument, then the truth or otherwise of Christian belief (part of the 'necessary truths of reason') has to be established by rational, theological or philosophical argument. It cannot be established by the historical record in the Bible (which can at best deal with 'the accidental truths of history').

Lessing and those who thought like him uncoupled history, including biblical history, from theology. In 1787 the Old Testament scholar J P Gabler was appointed to a professorship at the University of Altdorf and gave an inaugural address whose title proclaimed the new-found separation between the historical study of the Bible and Christian doctrine: 'On the proper distinction between biblical and dogmatic theology and the specific objectives of each'. Biblical critics could be free to question anything in the Bible, because they could claim that none of their conclusions would in any way call into question the real truths of Christianity. First in Germany, later in America and Britain, this argument gained ground and freed biblical criticism to draw radical conclusions about the Bible.

Religion is a matter of present experience

Building on the Enlightenment's uncoupling of theology from history, liberal Christians of the nineteenth century found an alternative base for theology in the present experience of the Christian, rather than in the historical narrative of the Bible.

F D E Schleiermacher (1768–1834) is usually credited with establishing this new movement in theology. He argued that religion is essentially 'a feeling of ultimate dependence'. Such a sense of dependence on a power beyond oneself can be nourished by the Scriptures but does not depend on the Scriptures. This sense is available to people of all times and all places, whether they have a Bible or not.

Liberal Christians who followed Schleiermacher were therefore prepared to face the challenges which biblical criticism and science were going to pose for Christian faith. If science could prove that the universe was not made in seven days, or that the sun could not have stood still for Joshua, this did not undermine faith, which now stood on a different basis. If biblical critics questioned whether Moses really wrote the first five books of the Bible, or whether the Acts of the Apostles was in fact written by a companion of Paul (both were in question by the mid nineteenth century), these doubts could be faced without fear. The Bible could be seen as the record of human experiences of the divine: the important thing about the Bible was what it conveyed about such experience, not whether it was factually and scientifically accurate.

The Bible should be read 'like any other book'

In the early nineteenth century the modern study of history was just beginning. Historians were starting to be more critical about their sources: did a particular story represent a biased point of view, or was a particular chronicle unreliable because it was written long after the event?

It was not long before biblical critics were applying the same kind of criteria to the Bible, and treating the narratives of the Old and New Testaments, not as a simple representation of exactly how things took place, but as *sources* from which a truer picture of events could be reconstructed.

This new approach to the Bible applied to both Testaments, but its impact was most radical on the reading of the Old Testament. Read as it stands, the Old Testament tells of the Exodus of Israel from Egypt, the giving of the covenant and Law to Moses at Sinai, then the conquest of the land, and the struggle by the prophets to encourage the people to keep the covenant down the centuries, until the eventual punishment of the people in the Exile in the sixth century BC. But from the late eighteenth century onwards, scholars began to notice a number of inconsistencies in the story. For example, some of the earliest prophets do not mention the covenant – Amos, to take one instance, criticised the people for many things, but not for breaking the covenant. Or what of the law commanding the people to centralise their worship on Jerusalem and to destroy the shrines in other places (Deuteronomy 12:1–3)? Great figures such as Samuel and Solomon offered sacrifice outside Jerusalem without seeming to be aware of the law in Deuteronomy, while Elijah complained to God precisely that the Israelites had pulled down the altars of his shrines around the country, as something they should *not* have done rather than something which God had commanded (1 Kings 19:10).

Faced with many such tensions in the story, readers could do one of several things. First, they could follow Origen's path and allegorise the problem passages – what is historically improbable is meant to teach a spiritual lesson. But this kind of interpretation seemed arbitrary and unrealistic: the Reformers of the sixteenth century had insisted on taking Scripture in its literal sense because they believed that the kind of allegorical interpretation which Origen pioneered allowed the interpreter to draw whatever meaning they wanted from the text (Calvin said they made it a 'nose of wax').

Second, they could attempt to harmonise the details and provide an explanation which took account of the apparent anomalies, weaving them back into the traditional story. This was the course taken by conservative critics who wanted to uphold the reliability of the Bible.

Third, they could take the anomalies and difficulties as the key to a new interpretation of the Old Testament. This was the course taken by the greater part of biblical scholarship. The most obvious solution to the 'problem' of Samuel, Solomon and Elijah's apparent ignorance of Deuteronomy is that they really were unaware of the book – it had not yet been written. Nineteenth-century scholars came to believe that the evidence of the Old Testament itself compelled them to conclude that Deuteronomy and the rest of the Law was written down at the *end*, not at the *beginning*, of Israel's history, and that in consequence the Old

Testament's account of Israel's history is very different from the way things actually happened. The Old Testament is a collection of sources from which the history may be reconstructed, but does not simply recount reliable history as we would understand it.

Biblical critics today do not slavishly follow what the nineteenth-century critics said and wrote. Things have moved on. But scholars today would argue strongly that the principles which nineteenth-century scholars stood for are still valid, that what they were doing was simply to investigate problems which were unavoidable, and (many would add) that Christian faith has nothing to fear from an honest and open-ended investigation of its Scriptures – in fact, those who belong to the Churches of the Reformation are merely continuing the Reformers' insistence on the primacy of Scripture in its literal sense when they investigate these features of the Bible (Barr, 1983, pp. 34–38).

Criticism and the inspiration of Scripture

In this extract, a recent author writing on the subject of Jesus and the gospels explains how he reconciles a critical approach to the gospels with a belief that they are inspired Scripture.

> If some readers wonder if all this 'criticism' really is compatible with belief in the Gospels as inspired books, the answer is clearly yes. Of course, we must carefully examine any given practitioner's use of each method, for at times much 'chaff' is mixed in with the 'wheat'. Nonetheless, the basic principles are not only sound, they are demanded if one believes in the accuracy of Luke's description of how he wrote [Luke 1:1–4]. Given the similarities among Luke, Mark and Matthew, and, to a lesser degree, John, it stands to reason that the other evangelists proceeded somewhat similarly. Gospel criticism is not inherently an alternative to belief in the inspiration of the texts, though it has been used that way by some radical critics. Rather, it is a study of the ordinary human means of writing that God's Spirit superintended so as to ensure that the final product was exactly what God wanted to communicate to his people (cf. 2 Peter 1:21). (Blomberg, 1997, p. 81)

EXERCISE

How helpful do you find this way of looking at the issues raised by biblical criticism?

If God's Spirit used 'ordinary human means of writing', does that mean that we can accept as valid in the Bible not just methods which would be acknowledged today (such as using sources), but also things which may have been 'ordinary means' in biblical times but would not be today (such as writing in someone else's name or altering one's sources)?

Faith and criticism today

Biblical criticism today is enormously diverse. The mainly historical concerns of the nineteenth century have given way to a greater interest in the literary forms of the biblical literature. Postmodern readings of the biblical text deny that there is a single 'meaning' to be extracted. The problems and opportunities posed by biblical criticism for Christian faith remain, however, pretty much as they were posed by nineteenth-century scholarship.

Responses to the critical challenge form a wide spectrum, but for convenience we can divide this spectrum up into three types of response.

Fundamentalist

'Fundamentalism' can mean many things. Here, I am taking it to refer to a movement of thought particularly associated with American Churches, which began in the early decades of the twentieth century and which is marked by a belief that the Bible is inerrantly true in all that it affirms or teaches, whether in matters historical, scientific or religious. (See Barr, 1977 for a strongly critical appraisal; Marsden, 1980 for a historical analysis; Boice, 1979 for an inside view; visit the internet site at www.religiousmovements.org, maintained by the University of Virginia, for connections to major fundamentalist websites.)

Fundamentalism in its stricter sense began with the publication of a series of books called 'The Fundamentals' between 1910 and 1915. These were intended to be a counterblast to the destructive effects of modern theology and of biblical criticism in particular. The fundamentalist movement gave expression to the concern of many Christian people that the unique status of the Bible was under threat from critics. Criticism seemed to be undermining confidence in the word of God, and the fundamentalist response was (and is) to defend the Bible as absolutely trustworthy and without error of any kind.

When we look at inspiration in the following chapter we will see a little more of the roots of this view. The results of it are that many people, especially in the United States, are committed to defending every statement of the Bible as completely without error of any kind. Wherever, on this view, modern science or biblical criticism suggest that things may not have happened just as the Bible says, then scientists and critics are wrong because they have started from unbelieving presuppositions.

Fundamentalists will be anxious to defend a 'literal' reading of the text (though some critics of the movement hold that they slip into non-literal readings to help them out of difficulties: see Barr, 1977). A fundamentalist, for instance, is likely to believe that the world was created by a succession of direct actions of God, as Genesis 1 states. The evidence from cosmology and from geology which suggests a longer time scale and a successive and evolutionary development is less reliable, in the fundamentalist view, than the plain, revealed word of God in the Scriptures. The site of the Biblical Creation Society on the internet (http://www.pages.org/bcs/index.html) will give you the flavour of this kind of argument.

Open criticism

The opposite end of the spectrum is occupied by the position of open criticism. On this view, the true nature of Scripture, as of any other phenomenon with which we are confronted, can be discerned by free and rational enquiry. Biblical studies is an academic subject like any other, and governed by the same laws of rationality, evidence and argument which apply in, say, history or anthropology. The scholar must be free to seek the truth about the Bible, as about anything else. In any case, if Christian faith is to be related to the Scriptures, it must be to the Scriptures as they actually are and not as we might imagine them to be.

📖 **Read Matthew 1:23.** Matthew here cites a passage from Isaiah (7:14):

'Look, the virgin shall conceive and bear a son, and they shall name him Emmanuel', and it is clear that as Matthew understood the passage it was a plain prophecy of the virginal conception of Jesus. But if you turn to a modern version of Isaiah 7:14, in most translations you will find 'young woman' in place of Matthew's 'virgin'. The Hebrew word used by Isaiah (*'almâh*) is not very precise, and many scholars believe that Isaiah was not pointing to a miraculous birth in the far future but to a normal birth in the near future: a young woman, already pregnant, will soon bear a son, and the things Isaiah is prophesying for Israel will happen 'before the child knows how to refuse the evil and choose the good' (Isaiah 7:16). The New International Version is alone among major translations in taking *'almâh* here as 'virgin', and it has been suggested that its choice of translation was guided by doctrinal considerations, that is, the wish to conform to Matthew's understanding of Isaiah (Rogerson, 1999, pp. 14–15).

EXERCISE

The point about Matthew 1:23 is not whether the Hebrew word really does mean 'virgin', or more generally 'young woman'. The real questions for our purposes are the following.

• Are we committed *in advance* to proving that Matthew was right to think that Isaiah 7:14 referred to a virgin, or are we are able to approach Isaiah with an open mind, and allow that Isaiah may have meant something different from the traditional Christian interpretation? Is the meaning of Isaiah 7:14 already determined and decided for us by Matthew's use of it, or can we come to our own conclusions?

• If we can come to our own conclusions, there will be further consequences, in this instance for our understanding of the virginal conception of Jesus. (Did the whole idea arise from a misunderstanding of Isaiah?)

Biblical seriousness

The term 'biblical seriousness' is used by David S Yeago (1997, p. 97) to describe a way of reading the Scriptures which does not ignore historical criticism, which makes use of critical understanding, but which does not assume that the 'real' meaning of the text was obscure before criticism came along and is only becoming clear now. Yeago's argument is that the kind of critical study we have been examining misses the point if it presumes to sit in judgement on the classic Christian understanding of the text. In fact, classic Christian doctrines about God and Christ offer the key to enter into 'the texture of scriptural discourse concerning Jesus and the God of Israel' (Yeago, 1997, p. 88). Yeago's argument is dense and repays close attention.

Another approach is that of Blomberg (1997), quoted above, who maintains that criticism rightly practised need not conflict with a reading of Scripture from the standpoint of faith, as long as one separates the 'wheat' of good interpretation from the 'chaff' of poor interpretation.

Both Yeago and Blomberg want to avoid the potential which 'open criticism' entails, of coming to unorthodox conclusions from biblical study. The difference between the two is that Yeago attempts to draw the sting of the historical-critical method, by saying that it is at best only a preparatory way of understanding the Bible before the real 'theological' reading can begin, while Blomberg seems to accept the historical-critical method, together with the potential risk that one may come across a difficulty which cannot be explained away as 'chaff'.

Conclusion

In every other department of human endeavour we expect free and rational enquiry to arrive at the truth. Does the same principle hold good in the case of the Bible, or is this a special case in which we know the answers in advance? That is the challenge of the critical method as it has grown up since the eighteenth century. If we are to live and commend our faith in a world which acknowledges the power of free and rational enquiry, do we need to *expose* the Bible to the same kind of enquiry, whatever the result? Do we need to *protect* the Bible from that sort of enquiry? Or do we need to *integrate* a faith-reading and a critical reading of the Bible, whatever the risks?

EXERCISE
📖 **Re-read Matthew 20:29–30 and Mark 10:46–47.**

Imagine that someone has come to you troubled by the discrepancy between these two accounts, and consider the following questions. ▶▶

> • Is your own approach to the problem any different now from what it was before you read this chapter?
> • Do any of the different ways of dealing with critical questions which you have met in this chapter offer any constructive help?

Further reading

Barr, J (1977), *Fundamentalism*, London, SCM.

Barr, J (1983), *Holy Scripture: canon, authority, criticism*, Oxford, Clarendon.

Blomberg, C (1997), *Jesus and the Gospels: an introduction and survey*, Leicester, Apollos.

Boice, J M (ed.) (1979), *The Foundation of Biblical Authority*, Glasgow, Pickering.

McGrath, A E (ed.) (1995), *The Christian Theology Reader*, Oxford, Blackwell.

Marsden, G M (1980), *Fundamentalism and American Culture: the shaping of twentieth-century evangelicalism 1870–1925*, New York, Oxford University Press.

O'Neill, J C (1991), *The Bible's Authority: a portrait gallery of thinkers from Lessing to Bultmann*, Edinburgh, T and T Clark.

Reventlow, H (1984), *The Authority of the Bible and the Rise of the Modern World*, London, SCM.

Rogerson, J (1984), *Old Testament Criticism in the Nineteenth Century: England and Germany*, London, SPCK.

Rogerson, J (1999), *An Introduction to the Bible*, London, Penguin.

Yeago, D S (1997 [first pub. 1993]), The New Testament and the Nicene Dogma: a contribution to the recovery of theological exegesis, in S F Fowl (ed.), *The Theological Interpretation of Scripture: classic and contemporary readings*, pp. 87-100, Oxford, Blackwell.

3. INSPIRATION: DIVINE WORD AND HUMAN WORD

Introduction

The first two chapters of this book have examined why the Bible has become a problem for Christian interpretation today. This chapter and the next two will look at what qualities Christians have traditionally claimed for the Bible, and how these claims can make sense today. In this chapter we deal in particular with the 'inspiration' of the Bible: we shall be asking how we can say of the Bible that it is both divine word (which Christians have always held it to be) and human word (which it manifestly is).

Reflecting on experience

Can you think of an example in your own experience when a passage from the Bible has struck you with particular force?

If this has been your experience, how did this take place: did it happen 'out of the blue' or were you prepared in some way for it? Was it in the course of a sermon? Were you reading on your own? If this has not been your experience, how do you react to people who claim that the Bible 'speaks' to them in this direct way?

📖 **Read Jeremiah 23:16–32.** This passage can be taken as typical of the Old Testament view of prophecy as a message ('word') from the Lord. The prophet's message need not be merely a prediction of the future. It is essentially an authentic presentation of what God wishes to say. Notice the criticism of prophets who have not 'stood in the council of the Lord' (v. 18) so as to hear what he is saying. This passage from Jeremiah is not specifically about written texts, but one traditional understanding of the inspiration of Scripture is that Scripture is a form of prophecy like this, resulting in a kind of direct oracle from God.

The problem of the divine inspiration of Scripture

When Christians say that the Bible is 'inspired', they do not mean the word in the sense that we might say that Shakespeare, for instance, is 'inspired': that he produced noble, profound and moving literature. The inspiration of Scripture is not a judgement on its quality as literature, but a statement of belief about its origins. Believing that the Bible is inspired means believing that God is in some way responsible for the production of its writings. It also means believing that God still speaks through these inspired texts.

Most Christians would wish to say that the Bible is special, and many would also want to express this special quality in terms of inspiration. But there is little agreement on what this 'inspiration' entails. In particular, there are debatable problems about the following aspects of biblical inspiration.

- What is inspired? Is it the *words* that are inspired by God or were the *authors* inspired to produce a message?
- How did inspiration work? Were the biblical writers conscious of being inspired?
- If the Bible is inspired by God, does this mean that it shares God's perfection? Is it, as some people would argue, 'inerrant' – incapable of being in error in any respect? If it is not inerrant, how do we discern which parts are correct and which are not?
- If Old and New Testaments are both inspired by God, how do they relate to each other?

The understanding of inspiration has been a particular problem for those in the Reformation tradition, for whom the Bible has been the major authority. In the Catholic tradition, attention has been given to the issue, but because biblical interpretation is integrated into the Church's teaching authority it is not such a pressing or urgent difficulty (Burtchaell, 1969; Vawter, 1972).

Protestants in the past two centuries have divided into 'liberal' and 'conservative' camps on the issue of inspiration.

'Liberal' Christians have generally drawn attention to the human qualities of Scripture. They would point out that the Bible was written by people in particular cultures and that it shares many of the assumptions of those cultures. It contains many helpful thoughts and ideas, but also many other things which are limited in scientific understanding, morally questionable and sometimes frankly incredible to modern people. The Bible is therefore as much human words about God as it is God's word to humanity. Some parts will remain helpful while others will be less so. 'Liberal' Christians will take a more open view of the kind of biblical criticism that we investigated in Chapter 2.

'Conservative' Christians would begin their account of the Bible with its divine origin. From such texts as 2 Timothy 3:16, the conservative will argue that God is the author of the Scriptures. By his Holy Spirit God inspired the words of the Bible. The more thoroughly conservative would argue that this authorship guarantees the absolute factual accuracy of every statement in Scripture (the 'inerrancy' view). Others might argue for 'infallibility' rather than 'inerrancy': that because Scripture is inspired by God, it will not let down anyone who relies on it for the purposes God intended. 'Conservative' Christians will be more hesitant about the kind of biblical criticism which we investigated in Chapter 2, or even hostile towards it.

A classic statement of the conservative position was that of B B Warfield. In an article published in 1915, he explored the statements and assumptions about Scripture contained in the New Testament, and in the course of his study expressed his conclusions in this way:

> Its [the Scripture's] authority rests on its divinity and its divinity expresses itself in its trustworthiness; and the New Testament writers in all their use of it treat it as what they declare it to be – a God-breathed document, which, because God-breathed, [is] through and through trustworthy in all its assertions, authoritative in all its declarations, and down to its last particular, the very word of God, His 'oracles'. (Warfield, 1948, p. 150)

EXERCISE
Is the quotation from Warfield a 'strong' statement of confidence in Scripture, and the grounds for confidence? Or is Warfield's argument vulnerable from its conclusion: if Scripture's trustworthiness 'in all its assertions' can be dented (the seven days of creation, for instance), does that affect confidence in its divine origin?

Compare Warfield's view with that of a well-known critic of fundamentalism, James Barr:

> Today, I think we believe, or have to believe, that God's communication with the men of the biblical period was not any different from the mode of his communication with his people today. 'Inspiration' would then mean that the God whom we worship was also likewise in contact with his people in ancient times, and that in their particular circumstances, in the stage in which they existed, he was present in the formation of their tradition and in the crystallization of that tradition as Scripture; but that the mode of this contact was not different from the mode in which God has continued to make himself known to men. (Barr, 1972, pp. 17–18)

EXERCISE

Does this extract from Barr say *enough* about inspiration? Do we know enough about how God is in contact with people today to say anything useful about how he may have been in contact with people of biblical times?

📖 **Read 2 Timothy 3:16.** This is the central text on inspiration in the Bible itself. We should note two important things about this passage. One is that many scholars do not believe it was written by Paul: the theology and language of 2 Timothy seems too far removed from Paul in, say, Galatians. The other is that the works referred to as 'Scripture' are far from clear – it must mean Old Testament books, since the New Testament had not yet been recognised as a collection of Scriptures, but it does not solve the problem of discerning which books have this property of 'inspiration'.

Warfield drew attention to the implications of 2 Timothy 3:16 for our understanding of the origin and nature of Scripture. Others have seen the emphasis of this text more in its 'tail': it is mainly urging the *usefulness* rather than defining the *God-givenness* of Scripture.

What is 'inspiration'?

Some recent interpreters of the concept of inspiration have appealed to the analogy with human inspiration. We can speak, for instance, of a teacher inspiring her or his pupils and students. In various ways, the example and work of teachers ignite a response among those with whom they are in contact, and while some grasp little more than the essentials, others penetrate further into the mind and heart of their teacher. In this kind of way we can explain what inspiration means, and how it is that some parts of the Bible seem to have a deeper under-standing of God than others (so Abraham, 1981– see below).

However, such a view starts with the range of meaning of the English word 'inspiration', rather than the Greek word by which the idea was first defined: *theopneustos*. This word means something like 'breathed out by God'. We have to recognise, therefore, that accepting the inspira-tion of the Scriptures in the traditional sense entails believing that the Holy Spirit was active in their production.

It is because they believe that the Scripture is inspired that many Christians want to describe the Bible as the word of God. If God has inspired it, this is as good as saying that God has spoken these, his words. This is the point at which difficulties begin to be apparent.

Why is inspiration a problem?

Laying aside the difficulties raised by arguments which build on inspiration to create further doctrines, for instance of inerrancy, the doctrine of the divine inspiration of Scripture itself raises several difficulties. Three in particular may be mentioned.

The difficulty of the phenomena of Scripture

By 'phenomena' here we mean the observed facts within the Bible. Some of these phenomena are moral difficulties: is it easy to believe that the command to kill all the inhabitants of the cities of Canaan, including the little children (Deuteronomy 20:16), was inspired by the same God who inspired Matthew 5:44's 'Love your enemies'? Some of the phenomena are errors (as it would seem to most people) at a factual level. Some 'errors' relate to the text's description of the external world. When geologists demonstrated to most people's satisfaction that the earth was not created in one day, it gave a lot of trouble to Christians who assumed that God said clearly that it had been (Genesis 1:9–10). On a different scale, Jesus states quite unequivocally that the mustard seed is 'the smallest of all the seeds on the earth' (Mark 4:31) which, taken as a statement of botanical fact, is not true. And finally, there are internal contradictions within the Bible. According to Paul, 23,000

Israelites died at Shittim, while the book of Numbers puts the figure at 24,000 (1 Corinthians 10:8 and Numbers 25:9). Did God inspire one writer to get the figure right and the other to get it wrong? Whatever understanding of inspiration one comes to, our view has to be able to encompass these kinds of observable facts about Scripture.

The writing of Scripture as a process, rather than an event

The traditional understanding of biblical inspiration assumed that each book had an author (Moses for the Pentateuch; individual prophets for the prophetic books; Matthew, Mark, Luke and John for the gospels and so on). A major shift, though, has taken place in biblical scholarship in the last century or so, and now the majority of scholars is convinced that the writing of many biblical books was only the final phase of a long process of development. Biblical scholars are also less sure today that we can always name the individuals who wrote each book. To take the creation stories in Genesis 1 and 2 as an example: a modern text book would point out the likelihood that the two stories of creation (Genesis 1:1 to 2:4a and 2:4b–25) were each created and handed down orally over a long period. The first story may have been used in Temple ritual. These two stories were placed together by a final editor of the Pentateuch at quite a late stage, perhaps as late as the fifth century BC. So where did inspiration happen? It was straightforward according to the old view: God revealed it all to Moses, who wrote it down. But according to the modern view, one might wonder whether it was just the final writer who was inspired, or was it the people who preserved the stories over the centuries, or was it the first originators, whoever they may have been? Our view of inspiration therefore will need either to reject the entire modern project of biblical studies (and produce good reasons for doing so), or put together an understanding which can see the writing of Scripture as a process rather than a series of events.

Canon

The problem of the canon is a long-standing one, and in the Reformation era Roman Catholic apologists used it as an argument against the Protestant reliance on Scripture alone. Scripture itself does not define what the limits of Scripture are, as we saw when looking at 2 Timothy 3:16 above. In the early Church there was disagreement for several centuries about the exact limits of the canon. If inspiration is seen as a quality which is present in certain works and not in others, then how do we decide what those works are? We shall return to consider the canon in more detail in later chapters.

How do we solve the problem?

Here are some suggested solutions to the problem posed by this doctrine.

- The whole idea of an inspired Bible is a mistake: the Bible is a human book, expressing the religious opinions (sometimes sublime, but often narrow and mistaken) of people who lived long ago.
- God revealed himself in certain events (such as the Exodus or the coming of Jesus), and the Bible is the record of human responses to this revelation. These responses are of varying quality.
- It would be better to say that God inspires the *readers* to perceive a message about God, rather than that God inspired the *writers* to set down a true message from him.
- The words of Scripture are the words given by God through the biblical writers, and if problems arise when we try to relate this belief to some of the things we find in the Bible, these problems are all capable of being resolved with good will and patience.
- The whole concept of inspiration (and of revelation) needs to be rethought.

EXERCISE

Think over each of the suggested solutions given above. What are the strengths and weaknesses of each?

Exploring solutions

Here are some proposed solutions to the problem of biblical inspiration, some of which expand on the ones given above.

God revealed himself in events, and Scripture is the human response to these events

This was a characteristic outlook of the 'biblical theology' movement of the middle years of the twentieth century. Although James Barr was highly critical of much of this movement, his understanding of inspiration seems to share something of this view of inspiration as human response:

Inspiration today can no longer mean historical accuracy or any sort of infallibility, nor can it be restricted to the mere writing down of Scripture by its supposed 'writers'. As we have seen, the communication and formation of what we now know as the Bible must extend over an enormous number of people, most of them anonymous. It must mean the inspiration, not of writers of books, but of the tradition of the believing community, out of which Scripture was eventually formed. It must mean that God was with his people in ancient time, in his Spirit, so that their responses to him were in adequate measure true and valid responses. 'Adequate' is as far as we can go in this, for the Bible is not theologically perfect, any more than it is necessarily historically accurate. (Barr, 1980, pp. 124–125)

God inspires the readers rather than the writers

Karl Barth was one of the most influential theologians of the twentieth century. His understanding of Scripture was as a witness to Christ. God revealed himself to human witnesses who then wrote the Scriptures: 'Revelation engenders the Scripture which attests it.' The Bible bears witness to past revelation. It is a human product, a human word, but Scripture can still be called the word of God because God graciously speaks to *us* through it. So God inspires the readers to perceive a message about him, rather than inspiring the writers to set down a true message from God.

The Bible is God's Word to the extent that God causes it to be His Word, to the extent that He speaks through it. . . . We cannot abstract from the free action of God in and by which he causes it to be true for us here and now that the biblical word of man is His own Word. The statement that the Bible is God's Word is a confession of faith, a statement of the faith which hears God Himself speak through the biblical word of man. . . . We accept it as a description of God's action in the Bible, whatever may be the experiences which we have or do not have in this connexion. . . . It does not become God's Word because we accord it faith but in the fact that it becomes revelation to us. (Barth, 1975, pp. 109–110)

The words of Scripture are the words given by God through the biblical writers

There have been a number of attempts to restate a traditional understanding of inspiration. Some have been fundamentalist assertions of the total identity of the words of the Scripture as words from God, which therefore share God's perfection. If a factual inaccuracy is accepted in the words of Scripture, it is as good as saying that God has lied. This view is strongly advocated by a large number of Protestant Christians, but is open to the kind of questioning which we looked at above (see: Why is inspiration a problem?).

Other writers, who have wanted to retain a traditional view of inspiration but also to do justice to the observable phenomena of Scripture (including the various styles of different books, the use of sources and so on), have proposed a notion of 'concursive inspiration'. That is, the process of writing the Scriptures may be seen from two points of view: from one, it is a fully human act, from the other, a divine activity. This next extract uses an analogy with creation, which is likewise a natural series of happenings but also, on a Christian view, a divine activity:

> On a human level we can describe its [the Bible's] composition in terms of the various oral and literary processes that lay behind it – the collection of information from witnesses, the use of written sources, the writing up and editing of such information, the composition of spontaneous letters, the committing to writing of prophetic messages, the collecting of the various documents together, and so on. At the same time, however, on the divine level we can assert that the Spirit, who moved on the face of the waters at Creation (Genesis 1:2), was active in the whole process so that the Bible can be regarded as both the words of men and the Word of God. This activity of the Spirit can be described as 'concursive' with the human activities through which the Bible was written. (Marshall, 1982, p. 42)

Inspiration today

Previous generations could accept that God had dictated the words of Scripture to his chosen instruments. Modern scholarship has created the problem of inspiration by drawing attention to the human processes involved in the writing of Scripture. How do you see a way of reconciling the tradition with modern insights? Fundamentalism reasserts the traditional position in defiance of modern scholarship, while radical positions on the other side regard Scripture as a more or less arbitrary collection of all-too-human writings. Is there a way of accepting divine inspiration in some sense *and* embracing a 'critical' reading of Scripture?

William Abraham explores the more everyday meaning of 'inspiration':

> Imagine for a moment a situation where we would naturally say that a teacher had inspired his students. Think of the light that this throws on the meaning of inspiration. We should note the following features as being essential to the description of the process. First, since the students will vary in their ability, temperament and interests, and since the intensity of their relationship may also vary, it is perfectly in order to speak of degrees of inspiration . . . Secondly, there is no question of the students remaining passive while they are being inspired. On the contrary: their natural abilities will be used to the full and as a result they will show great differences in style, content and vocabulary . . . Thirdly, as there will be other influences and sources of inspiration at work upon them, there need be no surprise if, from the point of view of the teacher, they make mistakes. (Abraham, 1981, pp. 63–64)

EXERCISE

This chapter has quoted six statements about the inspiration of Scripture (two by James Barr, one each by B B Warfield, I Howard Marshall, Karl Barth and W J Abraham). Note a strong feature and a weak point with respect to each of these six passages. Then evaluate the strengths and weaknesses you have identified.

Does any statement emerge as more convincing than the others – and if so, on what grounds?

Further reading

Abraham,W J (1981), *The Divine Inspiration of Holy Scripture*, Oxford, Oxford University Press.

Achtemeier, P J (1980), *The Inspiration of Scripture: problems and proposals*, Philadelphia, Westminster.

Barr, J (1972), *The Bible in the Modern World*, London, SCM.

Barr, J (1980), The Bible as a Document of Believing Communities, in Barr, *Explorations in Theology 7: the scope and authority of the Bible*, pp. 111–133, London, SCM.

Barth, K (1975, ET second edition [original German, 1932]), *Church Dogmatics 1: the doctrine of the word of God*, Vol. 1, Edinburgh, T and T Clark.

Berkouwer, G C (1975), *Holy Scripture*, ET Grand Rapids, Michigan, Eerdmans.

Boice, J M (ed.) (1979), *The Foundation of Biblical Authority*, Glasgow, Pickering.

Burtchaell, J T (1969), *Catholic Theories of Biblical Inspiration since 1810: a review and critique*, Cambridge, Cambridge University Press.

Marshall, I H (1982), *Biblical Inspiration*, London, Hodder and Stoughton.

Trembath, K R (1987), *Evangelical Theories of Biblical Inspiration: a review and proposal*, Oxford, Oxford University Press.

Vawter, B (1972), *Biblical Inspiration*, London, Hutchinson and Philadelphia, Westminster.

Warfield, B B (1948), The biblical idea of inspiration, reprinted in Warfield, *The Inspiration and Authority of the Bible*, pp. 131–166, Phillipsburg, New Jersey, Presbyterian and Reformed.

4. IS IT TRUE? THE BIBLE AND SCIENCE

Introduction

In this chapter, we shall be thinking particularly about the Bible and science, and so shall try to focus our attention on how the things we learn from the Scriptures can relate to what we learn from observation of our world. We are not discussing the wider problems of science and religion, although of course they impinge on our subject (see another book in this series, *God's World*, Astley, 2000, Chapter 5). The difficulty of relating the Bible and science is not just a matter of the details in Genesis 1 and 2, but of relating our thinking to a literature which comes to us from a culture very different from our own. So the Bible raises questions for us, not just about creation but also about miracle and providence, things accepted as evident possibilities in the ancient cultures from which the Bible comes, but disputed and less evident to people who see the world governed by known laws of physics.

Reflecting on experience
Have you experienced anything which you would describe as a 'miracle'? What do you consider a miracle to be? What would you think needs to happen to make an unusual occurrence into a miracle?

📖 **Read Mark 9:14–29.** We can take the incident recorded here as an example of a miracle story, and one for which modern people might give an alternative, non-miraculous explanation. Rudolf Bultmann (1884–1976), one of the most influential New Testament scholars of the twentieth century, was insistent that it was not just difficult but impossible for modern people to accept the idea of miracle as we find it in this text from Mark. The idea of such miracles only made sense in a pre-scientific age, when people simply assumed that the world was at the mercy of unseen spiritual forces. Now we assume that the world is governed by scientific laws – and since we accept the benefits of the progress of science we cannot pretend to accept the previous view of the world. In an important essay first published in 1941, he put the dilemma in these words:

> We cannot use electric lights and radios and, in the event of illness, avail ourselves of modern medical and clinical means and at the same time believe in the spirit and wonder world of the New Testament. And if we suppose that we can do so ourselves, we must be clear that we can represent this as the attitude of Christian faith only by making the Christian proclamation unintelligible and impossible for our contemporaries. (Bultmann, 1984, pp. 4–5)

EXERCISE

Taking the story you have just read from Mark's gospel as an example, does Bultmann's comment make you read it differently? Was this a misunderstood case of epilepsy, for instance? Was spirit possession something which happened then, but does not happen now? Or can we still believe in the 'spirit and wonder world of the New Testament'?

The problem of creation

4004 BC and all that

In 1650 Archbishop James Ussher of Dublin (1581–1656) calculated that the world had been created in 4004 BC. He was not more specific than that, but soon afterwards John Lightfoot (1602–1675), Vice-Chancellor of Cambridge University, made good Ussher's omission: Lightfoot improved on Ussher's figure by specifying the completion of creation at 9.00a.m. on Sunday 23rd October 4004 BC.

Ussher has been held up to ridicule for his pains, but in the terms of his own day what he did was quite reasonable. He arrived at his date by adding together all the indications of time in the Old Testament, so that he could work out how many years had elapsed from the creation of the world to the coming of Christ. He recognised that there was room for error in his figures, and did not claim absolute accuracy, but he considered that he was not far off the truth. For people of his generation, the sure facts of revealed Scripture were a more solid basis for reasoning than the doubtful observations and hypotheses of human ingenuity. Ussher's misfortune was to have lived just before the rise of modern science which reversed the order of these two sources of knowledge. Astronomers such as Galileo had already begun to demonstrate in the early seventeenth century the possibilities which scientific observation offered for altering our view of the world, but the success of scientific investigation across a wide field established in the eighteenth century the viability and soundness of scientific method, and swept all before it.

From the eighteenth century onwards, the Bible was placed in a new position. It was no longer the only source of information about the earth's remote past: science was beginning to come up with an alternative account. Within a generation of Ussher's death, his method was already looking rather quaint, and by the time two centuries had passed it had become a prime example of Christian opposition to science – although in his own time it was nothing of the kind.

Darwin and the Bible

The publication of Darwin's *The Origin of Species* in 1859 is one of the epoch-making events of the modern world. Darwin was not the first to propose that evolution of living things had taken place (his own grandfather had speculated along these lines). Nor was he the first to argue that the world was considerably older than a literal reading of the Bible would suggest – the first volume of Sir Charles Lyell's *Principles of Geology* was published in 1830, and had helped persuade many thoughtful people (Christians included) that geological time was vastly longer then they had imagined.

The difference with Darwin was that for the first time the idea of the evolution of species through natural selection was placed on a base of solid evidence. Darwin had gathered a mass of material through his wide reading and during his voyage on the ship HMS Beagle. He advanced his conclusions only after taking this huge body of evidence into consideration. No one could accuse him of jumping to conclusions with no warrant.

Darwin's work threw up difficulties for biblical interpretation in several respects:
• The evolution of species could be taken as a denial of the statement of

Genesis 1:21 and 24, that God created creatures 'according to their kinds'. Some Christian interpreters took (and take) this text to mean that species are fixed and do not evolve into other species.

- Genesis 1:26 was traditionally taken to imply that human beings, at least, were a special creation by God. Darwin realised that this was dangerous ground and he did not directly deal with it in *The Origin of Species*. He waited until he could gauge the strength of reaction before publishing his views on this last piece of the picture in *The Descent of Man* (1871). 'Men descended from apes?' mused the wife of a senior Victorian cleric. 'Let us hope it is not so. Or if it is, that it does not become widely known.' If there was no special creation of humanity, it seemed to undermine the dignity of human beings and make them little more than animals. If Adam was not a historical figure, then the Fall was not historical. If there was no Fall, then did mankind need a saviour after all?

- Darwin seemed finally to have taken the notion of *purpose* out of creation. Instead of a world carefully planned by a benevolent creator, Darwin appeared to offer a world of chance, in which everything could be explained by its origins, and nothing could be said to have a purpose.

EXERCISE
📖 **Read Genesis 1:26–31.**

Is the most important aspect of this passage how humanity was created or why it was created? Can science ever give an account of purpose, such as these verses provide?

The biblical world-view and the Bible's message

The challenge of the scientific account

The people who wrote the Bible probably did not have very clear ideas about the shape and size of the earth, whether the sky was solid or whether the abode of the dead was to be found under the earth beneath their feet. So when they make statements about the world, do we need to accept what they say? Did divine inspiration keep them from making any scientific mistakes? Or should we approach the Bible assuming that its writers were people of their time, with all its scientific limitations, and try to disentangle the *message* they preached from the *world-view* they assumed?

This problem is not a new one. It surfaced as soon as western science began to discard the world-view which the biblical writers had lived with, and that process of discarding the older world-view started to take place in the sixteenth century.

Disentangling the biblical world-view: early astronomy

Astronomy caused difficulties for biblical interpretation well before biology did so. In the sixteenth and seventeenth centuries, astronomical observations were beginning to make it seem likely that the earth rotated around the sun (the heliocentric theory) rather than the sun around the earth (the geocentric theory). In these circumstances theologians had to face the question of whether the Bible was making a *positive affirmation* about the physical structure of the universe when it said, for example, that the sun 'comes out like a bridegroom from his wedding canopy, and like a strong man runs its course with joy' (Psalm 19:5), and that the sun stood still in its course for Joshua (Joshua 10:12). Was the geocentric world-view of the scriptural writers simply the common imagery of their times, or did its appearance in the Bible necessarily give it the sanction of something revealed by God? The Bible seems to *assume* an earth-centred universe, but does that mean that it was *teaching* an earth-centred universe?

In 1616 the Roman Catholic Church ordered Galileo to cease teaching that the earth moves around the sun. The reasons for Galileo's condemnation were complex but rested to some degree on questions of biblical interpretation and Church politics: Galileo's theory required that the Church should interpret the Scriptures in a novel manner, and if it did that it would be admitting that the Church's traditional interpretation had been wrong and so might give too much ammunition to the Protestants (McGrath, 1998, pp. 207–213). Galileo and his supporters were confident that the apparently geocentric statements in Scripture were simply pictorial language and that the essential teaching of Scripture did not depend on the scientific accuracy of statements about the sun moving across the sky (McMullin, 1998, pp. 277–278). They were doing in the seventeenth century what Bultmann was to try to do in the twentieth: to distinguish the culturally outmoded *way* in which Scripture is expressed from the enduring *message* which the Scriptures express.

Demythologising

The extract from Rudolf Bultmann which appeared earlier in this chapter is one aspect of Bultmann's argument that the scientific view of the biblical writers (and indeed their entire outlook on the world) is no part of the Bible's real message. In his view, it is possible to reinterpret the features in the Bible which belong to this outmoded outlook on the world (such as miracles and spirits) and reveal afresh the true meaning of the Scriptures. In Bultmann's thinking, this meaning was a challenge to decision in response to the preached message of the early Church.

Bultmann did not intend to discard or denigrate what the New Testament had to say about miracle or about spiritual beings, but he was convinced that these things were simply another culture's way of talking about realities of experience which we have to talk about in different terms. This reinterpretation applied equally to the resurrection of Jesus: we cannot in a scientific age believe in a corpse being returned to life, and all we can do with the Easter stories is say that they expressed the subjective experience and belief of the disciples, not the objective facts about an event. He saw this as a process of taking the mythical elements in Scripture and reinterpreting them in terms of experienced realities, and he called it *demythologising*.

The New Testament writers, in Bultmann's view, intended to challenge people to respond to the preached message of Jesus, and to achieve this they had to speak in terms of their own culture. But we, equally, have to speak in terms of *our* culture, so we have to 'translate' their talk of angels, demons, spirits and miracles into terms and language which make sense to our scientific age.

EXERCISE

Bultmann has been enormously influential as an interpreter who took seriously the gap between the modern world-view and the ancient. But he has also been criticised for capitulating too readily to a supposed modern world-view which sees reality as a closed system of cause and effect. The following are some questions to consider concerning Bultmann's method and conclusions.

- Was he right that modern people find belief in, say, miracle impossible?
- Are biblical accounts of miracle merely using the assumptions of the surrounding culture, or are they intending to affirm ▶▶

> something about the relation between God and the world – and
> if so, is the view of the world as a closed system of cause and
> effect one to which Christians cannot subscribe?
> • Is a Christian faith without belief in the resurrection as an objec-
> tive event (however vaguely defined) still essentially *Christian*?
> See 1 Corinthians 15:12–19.

The fundamentalist interpretation

The fundamentalist approach represents the opposite of Bultmann's
view: it *maximises* the extent to which the Bible 'teaches' scientific
truths, while Bultmann *minimised* the information-giving aspect of the
Bible and regarded all biblical statements about the world (heaven
above, hell below, constant interference by spirits and so on) as part of
the cultural baggage of the biblical world-view.

We have already seen, when considering the inspiration of Scripture,
the reasons for the fundamentalist view. It is based on a belief that the
words of Scripture are God's words, and therefore express God's com-
prehensive knowledge of the world, its structure and history. In 1978,
at a meeting to consider the nature of the Bible, a group of fundamentalists issued the 'Chicago Statement on Biblical Inerrancy', which
remains a good explanation of the fundamentalist position. In the summary of their position, the Group declared the following (point 4 of the
statement summary): 'Being wholly and verbally God-given, Scripture
is without error or fault in all its teaching, no less in what it states about
God's acts in creation ... than in its witness to God's saving grace in
individual lives.'

Fundamentalists who simply insist that modern science is wrong in
certain respects (such as the age of the earth or the possibility of evolution of species) and who take their stand on the Bible alone have a consistent case. The problem with their position is that they live, as
Bultmann pointed out, in a world in which every other part of their
lives is shaped by modern science and technology. To ease the tension
between what they believe about Scripture (that it contradicts the
findings of science) and what they experience about the world (that
science works rather well), many fundamentalists attempt to argue on
scientific grounds that Scripture is, after all, correct.

The Biblical Creation Society, for instance, exists 'to think through
issues related to origins from a coherent biblical and scientific stand-

point' (The Biblical Creation Society's website can be found on the internet at: http://www.pages.org/bcs/index.html). But if a modern 'creationist' succeeds in demonstrating the coherence of the Bible with contemporary science, they have only succeeded in linking Scripture with one phase of scientific development. Why give priority to present-day science? As Paul Achtemeier put it:

> If Scripture is in fact free from error in the form in which it purveys divine truth, it must be free from such error not only for the time for which it was written but also for future times in which it will be read. Scripture therefore must be recognizably as free from error to the medieval scientist searching for the way to transmute base metal into gold as it must be free from error to the modern physicist seeking a field theory of physical forces, despite the widely differing presuppositions each brings to Scripture about the nature of the physical world. If truth is one, and the Bible as truth must exclude error, on whose presuppositions is that truth to be explained, the alchemist's or the modern physicist's? Whose presuppositions will determine, for example, what is the actual view in the Bible of geography, or geology, or botany, or the process of creation? The fact that this problem is seldom if ever discussed by conservatives points to a naive absolutizing of our current level of scientific theory and knowledge on the part of conservatives. (Achtemeier, 1980, pp. 96–97)

In the scientific as well as in the historical arena, thorough-going fundamentalism needs, at the very least, to be sustained by a constant and ever-vigilant apologetic.

The purpose of Scripture

In the next chapter, we will consider whether modern readers make a mistake by jumping to the conclusion that the Bible always narrates history as we understand it when it tells a story such as that of Noah's ark. If biblical narrative is not always history as we understand it, then we would be wrong either to judge it as 'unhistorical' and so false, or to attempt to defend its account as though it *were* modern-style history. It is important and helpful to take into account the *purpose* of Scripture. Something similar applies to reading the Bible in a scientific age and trying to match its statements with a scientific account of the world.

Goldingay (1994) has argued that it is a mistake to jump from the *belief* that all Scripture is inspired to the *conclusion* that it is therefore inerrant. The key to understanding inspiration in this context is that this doctrine affirms that the words of Scripture are effective and meaningful, like the words of prophecy. Like prophetic words, scriptural words bring about those things of which they speak and have a meaning which goes beyond their original context (Goldingay, 1994, pp. 209–221). The biblical writers worked within the limits of the information available to them, including their own memories (1 Corinthians 1:14–16), and presumably therefore also within the limits of their own education. In any event: 'As S T Coleridge remarks, there is no reason to believe that the biblical writers were "divinely informed as well as inspired" (Confessions 27 (Letter 2))' (Goldingay, 1994, p. 280).

In fact, taking the purpose of Scripture into account when trying to match it against a scientific account of the world is nothing new. In the following passage, St Basil the Great (c. 330–379) reflects on the interface of science (as he knew it) and Scripture in the matter of creation.

> Those who have written about the nature of the universe have discussed at length the shape of the earth. If it be spherical or cylindrical, if it resemble a disc and is equally rounded in all parts, or if it has the form of a winnowing basket and is hollow in the middle; all these conjectures have been suggested by cosmographers, each one upsetting that of his predecessor. It will not lead me to give less importance to the creation of the universe, that the servant of God, Moses, is silent as to shapes; he has not said that the earth is a hundred and eighty thousand furlongs in circumference; he has not measured into what extent of air its shadow projects itself whilst the sun revolves around it, nor stated how this shadow, casting itself upon the moon, produces eclipses. He has passed over in silence, as useless, all that is unimportant for us. Shall I then prefer foolish wisdom to the oracles of the Holy Spirit? Shall I not rather exalt Him who, not wishing to fill our minds with these vanities, has regulated all the economy of Scripture in view of the edification and the making perfect of our souls? (Basil, *Hexaemeron* 9)

EXERCISE

What did Basil consider to be the purpose for which God had given Scripture? He was ready to dismiss the science of his day as 'vanity', whereas today we are in the opposite situation – today ▶▶

most people regard science as enormously useful while 'theology' is sometimes used to describe arcane and useless speculation! But do Basil's words help us to form our own view (in the changed circumstances of our own time) on the respective purposes of Scripture and science?

Further reading

Achtemeier, P J (1980), *The Inspiration of Scripture: problems and proposals*, Philadelphia, Westminster.

Barbour, I G (1998), *Religion and Science: historical and contemporary issues*, London, SCM.

Bultmann, R (1984), *New Testament and Mythology: and other basic writings*, London, SCM.

Chadwick, O (1975), *The Secularization of the European Mind in the 19th Century*, Cambridge, Cambridge University Press.

Chicago Statement on Biblical Inerrancy: on the internet at http://www.iclnet.org/pub/resources/text/history/chicago.stm.txt.

Goldingay, J (1994), *Models for Scripture*, Grand Rapids, Michigan, Eerdmans and Carlisle, Paternoster.

McGrath, A (1998), *Historical Theology: an introduction to the history of Christian thought*, Oxford, Blackwell.

McMullin, E (1998), Galileo on science and Scripture, in P Machamer (ed.), *The Cambridge Companion to Galileo*, pp. 271–347, Cambridge, Cambridge University Press.

Moore, J R (1979), *Post-Darwinian Controversies 1870–1900*, Cambridge, Cambridge University Press.

5. DID IT HAPPEN? THE BIBLE AND HISTORY

Introduction

In Chapter 2 we looked at Origen's approach to biblical interpretation in the third century, and noted that he believed that the Bible could sometimes express spiritual truth while being factually in error. We went on to look at the ways in which a number of theologians and biblical critics since the Enlightenment have pursued a similar course, and have attempted to uncouple the religious value of the Bible from its factual reliability. We have seen that many modern interpreters can argue that the Scriptures contain an important *spiritual* message, even if (they maintain) modern people can no longer accept all its statements as *factually* true.

If we follow that course, it becomes easier to make sense of the Bible in a modern setting – even in what is being called our 'postmodern' culture. Lesslie Newbigin identified one of the characteristics of present-day western culture as the separation of 'fact' and 'value': we often unthinkingly accept that certain areas of experience deal with matters of 'fact' which can be established objectively as either right or wrong, while in other areas lie questions of 'value' in which one person's opinion is as good as another's, and in which there can be no question of right or wrong. Newbigin argued that our culture has moved religion from the realm of 'fact' to that of 'value'. So if we distinguish the spiritual message in the Scriptures (value) from its historical and scientific accuracy (fact), we are taking part in the cultural shift which Newbigin has described (Newbigin, 1986, pp. 15–20).

The following quotation is a candid expression of this way of interpreting the Scriptures as expressions of value rather than repositories of fact. The authors have just discussed modern scholarly understandings of the gospels, which see the gospels as expressing distinct theological positions: 'It turns out that, even as we found the gospels to be literary works whose intent is to convey a message rather than to present a factual account of historical events, the Bible as a whole is literature that deals with meaning rather than fact' (Ord and Coote, 1994, p. 91).

Reflecting on experience

How do you respond to the idea put forward in the previous quotation from Ord and Coote, that the Bible 'deals with meaning rather than fact'? Is it disturbing to think that the Bible is not essentially or necessarily factual – or is this idea liberating?

Do you think that the authors are right when they suppose that the Bible can still have meaning for us if it does not present us with facts?

The issues

Christianity is a historical faith. This means that it arises out of a story from the past, the story of Israel and the story of Jesus. In this respect the issue of the historical truth of the Bible is more telling and urgent than the problem of relating the Bible's world-view with modern science. It may be argued in the case of science that the *purpose* of Scripture is not to communicate scientific truths. But it does appear to be the purpose of large parts of the Bible to narrate history, and this history is crucial to Christian faith. Without the Exodus or without the story of Jesus, Christianity would not be what Christians down the ages have believed it to be.

If we then ask the question of whether this story is true, we are asking two questions in one.

- First, we are asking whether it is necessary for the Christian faith that the story it tells is historically accurate – for instance, in what sense is it the case that Jesus rose from the dead?
- Second, we are asking whether it is necessary for the Bible to be an accurate record of those stories – for instance, does it affect the Bible's value for us if Matthew was wrong about the number of donkeys on which Jesus rode into Jerusalem?

The first of these issues is a very important theological question which, as we saw in Chapter 2, was raised in the eighteenth century by Lessing: do theological truths depend on historical facts? But it is the second issue which will concern us in this chapter and the next, because it relates more directly to the Bible and its nature.

EXERCISE
📖 **Read 1 Corinthians 15:12–19.**

In this passage, Paul links the validity of Christian faith to the resurrection of Jesus: 'If Christ has not been raised . . . your faith has been in vain.' Many Christians would believe that it is essential to take the resurrection as a historical event – at least in some sense. But how far does that essential historical core of events related in the Scriptures extend? Jesus, in Matthew 12:38–41, draws a parallel between the three days and three nights which the 'Son of Man' would spend in the heart of the earth, and the three days and three nights which Jonah spent in the belly of the whale. If we believe that Jesus rose from the dead is it, therefore, necessary to believe that Jonah was swallowed by the whale? Is Christian faith 'in vain' if Jonah turns out to be fictional?

Biblical inerrancy

We have already come across the phenomenon of fundamentalism. To the fundamentalist (as we have defined the term) it is very important that the Bible should be without errors of any kind, because (theologically) it is the word of God and therefore shares his perfection, and (practically) it is the source of faith and any uncertainty about its statements would leave the believer without a solid foundation for faith. The fundamentalist would use a type of 'slippery slope' argument to defend this second point: if you concede that the story of Jonah might be fictional, or that Noah's ark might be a myth, what is going to prevent you following this logic through and ending up by concluding that the resurrection of Jesus never happened? So it is all or nothing: either every statement of Scripture is accepted as factually accurate or every statement is potentially unreliable and untrue.

The belief that everything the Bible states is factually accurate is summed up by saying that the Bible is 'inerrant'. In the previous chapter we came across the 'Chicago Statement on Biblical Inerrancy' of 1978, which offers a good explanation of what is meant by calling the

Bible 'inerrant'. In the summary of their position, the Group declared the following (points 4 and 5 of the statement summary):

4. Being wholly and verbally God-given, Scripture is without error or fault in all its teaching, no less in what it states about God's acts in creation, about the events of world history, and about its own literary origins under God, than in its witness to God's saving grace in individual lives.

5. The authority of Scripture is inescapably impaired if this total divine inerrancy is in any way limited or disregarded, or made relative to a view of truth contrary to the Bible's own; and such lapses bring serious loss to both the individual and the Church.

The inerrantist, in other words, would not accept that the Bible deals only with 'meaning'. It sets out facts. Nor would it be enough to say that it is theologically and morally 'reliable', but that historically and scientifically it reflects the limitations of the people who wrote it. The Bible (on this view) invariably states true facts about 'God's acts in creation' and about 'the events of world history'.

Is the Bible inerrant?

This kind of view no doubt holds a great attraction for many Christians – even those who are not committed to a totally fundamentalist outlook. It does, after all, make the Bible seem secure, and keeps our interpretation away from the slippery slope which might begin with apparently trivial concessions (Jonah's whale and Matthew's donkeys) and might end up with serious scepticism about central aspects of the faith (the resurrection of Jesus).

So, does the inerrantist view offer a safeguard against a slide down a slippery slope? Many people object to the fundamentalist and inerrantist position because they take issue with its entire outlook and 'mindset' (Barr, 1984; Boone, 1989). There are also problems specifically to do with the inerrantist's understanding of 'truth' in the Scriptures. Here are three of these problems.

• In Chapter 3 we noticed some of the observable facts about Scripture which do suggest that there are factual inaccuracies in the Bible. Inerrantists can take account of these by arguing that, for instance, scriptural writers dealt in round numbers (so explaining the discrepancy between 1 Corinthians 10:8 and Numbers 25:9), and that we should recognise exaggeration for rhetorical effect, as in Mark 4:31.

But maintaining the inerrantist case entails constant vigilance (and perhaps constant anxiety) in the face of the possibility that one day some detail will come to light which cannot be accommodated or explained in this kind of way, and the whole case will collapse – always a risk with 'all-or-nothing' arguments.

- The inerrantist seems to assume that the truth of the Bible is something which can be established objectively, in a way which would satisfy anyone, whether they approach it in faith or not. Hence the energy expended on defending 'creationism' with scientific arguments, or on locating the remains of Noah's ark. But is the 'truth' of the Scriptures something which can be recognised apart from faith? The Reformer John Calvin thought not: 'Those who wish to prove to unbelievers that Scripture is the word of God are acting foolishly, for only by faith can this be known' (Calvin, *Institutes* 1, 8, 13).

- Inerrantists assume that there is only one kind of 'truth': factual accuracy. Scripture is therefore a revelation of true facts or propositions about God. This concept of 'truth' needs to be examined more closely.

EXERCISE
📖 **Read Luke 15:11–32.**

Is this story true? What do you mean by 'true' here?

In thinking this through you might bear some other questions in mind.

- Can it be 'true' in some sense even if Jesus was not telling a story about an actual family and its history?

- If the story is 'true' (in what it says about God's love, for instance), even if it is possibly 'false' as a historical narrative, then was Jesus telling a lie by recounting a story of something that never really happened?

- If we think that recounting a parable is a legitimate way of conveying a true message, then might the same thing be said of other forms of communication, such as 'myths'? Could the stories of Jonah or Noah also convey a true message, even if they do not recount things that 'really happened'?

What is truth?

Literary forms

In thinking about the parable of the Prodigal Son in the previous exercise, we had to consider the literary form of the parable. Most people would agree that it is not important to be certain whether or not there really was a family like that described by Jesus, or for that matter whether there ever was a woman who lost a coin, or a farmer fortunate enough to enjoy the remarkable crops described in Mark 4:8. The 'truth' of a parable lies in its message, not in the story which conveys the message.

What about other literary forms in the Bible? Could there be other kinds of writing in the Bible in which what appear to be straightforward stories about things which happened in the past could in fact (like parables) be nothing of the kind? What about myth, for instance? We have to be careful about definitions here, because in normal English usage 'myth' can simply mean a made-up story, and this negative use is also found in the New Testament (for example, 2 Timothy 4:4). But 'myth' has a technical meaning in biblical studies for a story 'that has as its main actors superhuman beings and that is typically set in other-worldly time and space', and for narratives which 'through the use of symbolic language, communicate transcendent meaning within a culture, revealing its cosmic dimensions' (Susan Ackerman, in Metzger and Coogan, 1993, p. 539; see also Evans, 1999, pp. 78–79).

There is one obvious passage of the Bible which fits this description, and that is the creation story of Genesis 1:1 to 2.4a, which we considered in the previous chapter. However, many scholars would accept that much of Genesis 1 to 11 is 'mythical' in the sense that its stories are not intended to be set in 'real time', or to be read as historical accounts of things as they happened. They are symbolic stories that reveal the reasons for the way things *are*, rather as parables reveal the way things *could be*. For our consideration of what 'truth' might mean in this type of story, we will take an example of a well-known narrative from the early section of the Old Testament, Noah and his flood.

EXERCISE
📖 **Read Genesis 6:5 to 8:22.**

Was this story *intended* to be understood as straightforward reporting of facts?

There are several indications that it was not intended to be understood factually.

- Intrinsic probability: a flood which covered Mount Everest (Genesis 7:19–20) is hard for us to envisage, though for ancient Hebrews who believed the world was suspended between great reservoirs of water above and beneath, it was quite easy to think that the world would be destroyed if these reservoirs were broken open (Genesis 7:11).
- Internal difficulties: feeding the animals and dealing with their droppings would have posed problems, and individual species would have had their own difficulties, such as the dodo which had somehow to make its way from Mount Ararat to the island of Mauritius, despite being unable to fly! Nineteenth-century critics pointed out these and other anomalies (Rogerson, 1984, pp. 226–227).
- Comparative studies: the biblical story is similar to myths told in other cultures of the ancient Near East about a universal flood – if we do not consider it necessary to read the ancient Babylonian stories as historically accurate, why should the biblical story be different?
- These and other considerations lead most scholars to conclude that the Noah story is a myth:

> We are dealing with a narrative of primeval time that is in the context of the story of the creation of humans. Side-by-side with the creation of humanity there is now the possibility of its destruction; this leads to the preservation of humankind by saving the one. The creation of humans and their preservation involve a catastrophe; but the saving action does not take place in the realm of the history of humanity. It is an event that precedes history. (Westermann, 1984, p. 395)

EXERCISE

An 'inerrantist' would insist that there *must have been* a flood and an ark as described in Genesis, otherwise Scripture is saying something which is not true. But consider the following.

- If this story is myth and not history, then does its 'truth', like the truth of a parable, lie in its message?
- If we try to turn it into history (in our understanding of the word), are we in fact distorting the story?
- Do we first need to ask what the storyteller really *intended*?

How would you answer these questions?

The meaning of 'error'

So far, we have not paid attention to the question of what we mean by 'error'. We will be saying something different about the Bible if we attribute to it 'error' in the sense of intentional deceit, rather than 'error' as a factual slip. G C Berkouwer pointed out the danger of confusing the two, as he maintained was done in the 'inerrantist' argument:

> The concept of error in the sense of incorrectness is obviously being used on the same level as the concept of erring in the sense of sin and deception. The distinction is left rather vague. As a consequence of this, limited historical perception within a certain cultural and scientific situation is, without further stipulation, put on a par with erring in the sense of lying, the opposite of truth. If erring is formalized in this way, it cannot later be related to truth in a biblical sense, but it continues to function as a formal structure of exactness and correctness. Thus, we are quite far removed from the serious manner with which erring is dealt in Scripture. For there what is meant is not the result of a limited degree of knowledge, but it is a swerving from the truth and upsetting the faith (2 Timothy 2:18). (Berkouwer, 1975, p. 181)

Berkouwer suggests that the fundamentalists' mistake is to be so concerned with the *divine* aspect of Scripture, that they neglect for practical purposes its *human* aspect, the fact that it is inevitably expressed in human words. The fundamentalist supposes that the divine origin of Scripture, its God-breathed quality (2 Timothy 3:16), must guarantee that it expresses God's total knowledge, and that if it is shown to fall short of that (by telling mythical stories of events which did not happen, for instance) then its divine origin is disproved. Conversely, since it expresses God's total knowledge, then what it states (about the creation or Noah's flood, for example) *must* be a plain statement, as we would understand it, of what actually took place.

If, on the other hand, we take seriously the human aspect of a passage of Scripture, then we have to say that simply in order to be understood, the passage *had* to be put in terms which related to the culture in which it was written. No matter how great a part we ascribe to God in the production of Scripture, God still had to use human language and therefore human thought-forms and a scientific understanding related to particular cultures. For the scriptural writers to have made use of myth instead of modern history, or to have thought in terms of a 'three-decker universe' rather than a heliocentric solar system, is no more an error (for our purposes) than to have spoken in Hebrew rather than in English.

The purpose of Scripture

The Roman Catholic scholar Hans Küng, in his study of infallibility (written in the first instance with reference to the Roman Catholic Church's claim to infallible authority, but having a bearing on Scripture too), has proposed that the notion of 'infallibity' should be replaced by a notion of 'indefectibility'. By this term Küng means that the Church (or Scripture) is not always kept free from error, whether factual, moral or doctrinal, but that Church and Scripture do not ultimately fail in the purpose for which they have been given. 'Infallibility', Küng points out, really should refer to trustworthiness, to something which will not fail when you depend upon it, rather than to 'immaculateness' or 'faultlessness' (Küng, 1994).

Some people might think that Küng does not go far enough in asserting the trustworthiness of the Scriptures, but his approach opens up a different way of investigating what the 'truth' of the Scriptures might be. Such an approach might start by agreeing that a Bible passage is God-given, inspired and God-breathed (2 Timothy 3:16) but then, rather than deducing the qualities which such a God-breathed Scripture must have (such as sharing God's all-knowing view of reality), it would ask what God's purpose might have been in inspiring the Scripture. If that purpose is 'to instruct you for salvation through faith in Christ Jesus' (2 Timothy 3:15), then this approach could then ask what qualities the passage should have to accomplish this purpose. For this purpose, it does not need (presumably) to be factually accurate or inerrant in every historical or scientific statement. In order to fulfil the purpose of instructing us for salvation through faith in Jesus Christ, it needs to be a fully trustworthy guide for those who in faith look for such instruction.

In the next two quotations, the idea of Scripture's trustworthiness is developed along the lines suggested in the previous paragraphs:

> Now the crucial point here is the concept of what God *wished* to be written. Our ideas of what *we* might have wished God to write may not be the same as what *he* may have wished to write. If we look once again at 2 Timothy 3:15f. we find that the stated purpose of the Scriptures is to provide the instruction that leads to salvation through faith in Jesus Christ, and this is then detailed in terms of teaching, reproof,

correction and training which enable the man of God to be fully equipped for every good work. The purpose of God in the composition of the Scriptures was to guide people to salvation and the associated way of life. From this statement we may surely conclude that God made the Bible all that it needs to be in order to achieve this purpose. It is in this sense that the word 'infallible' is properly applied to the Bible. (Marshall, 1982, p. 53)

In order to play their part in drawing us to trust in Christ, the Scriptures must give adequate testimony to the facts about him. To affirm that the Bible offers us adequate testimony is not to affirm that its narratives are inerrant. In a court of law and in other contexts where testimony matters, we are dependent on the general reliability of witnesses, and in the absence of general reliability we are at sea. But we are not dependent on witnesses making no mistakes, nor are we troubled when they contradict each other over certain matters. The concept of witness carries within it the notion of general reliability, but not that of inerrancy. Belief that Scripture is entirely adequate witness neither necessitates nor justifies belief in its factual inerrancy. (Goldingay, 1994, p. 45)

EXERCISE

Is the Bible True? This was the title of a book cited towards the beginning of this chapter. We could take it as a question to focus and clarify our thinking at this point: is the Bible true? The following are some possible answers that we have come across in the chapter. What do you now see as the strengths and weaknesses of each? Which do you find most credible – or is there another possibility altogether?

- The Bible is in many respects true for me – it expresses many values with which I want to identify (and some I do not).
- The Bible is entirely true in everything it states, whether on doctrinal, moral, scientific or historical matters – any difficulties can ultimately be explained.
- The Bible is entirely reliable for the purposes for which God intended it, but it should not be pressed to give answers in areas for which it was not intended.

Further reading

Barr, J (1984), *Escaping from Fundamentalism*, London, SCM.

Berkouwer, G C (1975), *Studies in Dogmatics: Holy Scripture*, Grand Rapids, Michigan, Eerdmans.

Boone, K C (1989), *The Bible Tells Them So: the discourse of Protestant fundamentalism*, London, SCM.

Ferguson, D S (1986), *Biblical Hermeneutics: an introduction*, Atlanta, John Knox and London, SCM (especially pp. 40–64).

Küng, H (1994), *Infallible? an unresolved enquiry*, London, SCM.

Marshall, I H (1982), *Biblical Inspiration*, London, Hodder and Stoughton.

Metzger, B M and Coogan, M D (eds) (1993), *The Oxford Companion to the Bible*, Oxford, Oxford University Press.

Newbigin, L (1986), *Foolishness to the Greeks*, London, SPCK.

Rogerson, J (1984), *Old Testament Criticism in the Nineteenth Century: England and Germany*, London, SPCK.

Westermann, C (1984), *Genesis 1–11*, London, SPCK.

6. DEFINING THE OLD TESTAMENT

Introduction

This chapter and the next are dealing with two sets of issues, and it is helpful to distinguish them before we begin. The first set is a group of *historical* questions: the process by which first the Jewish people and then the Christian Church came to recognise certain books as Scripture. The second set arises out of the first and is more directly *theological*: if the compilation of our Bible was a process, and was only completed after the biblical books had been written, how does this fact affect our view of the status of the Bible? For instance, if *the Church* eventually recognised the 27 books of the New Testament as its authoritative Scripture, does this mean that the Church has an authority over the Bible, and that it could in principle have recognised other books if it chose?

This second set of issues raises questions which go to the heart of our understanding of what the Bible is. But if we are to see clearly why these issues are important, we have first to get some idea of the historical picture and of how we have ended up with the Bible which we have.

The questions dealt with in these two chapters centre on the 'canon', so it will also help to be clear what we are talking about when we speak of 'Scripture' and 'canon'.

- 'Scripture' is a text which a believing community accepts as authoritative – to be used liturgically, or to be appealed to in matters of faith or doctrine.
- 'Canon' is a list of Scriptures which the believing community accepts as defining what is and what is not 'Scripture'. It is possible for a community to have 'Scriptures', but within an open-ended and still-growing canon.

Reflecting on experience

Have you been to a church service which included readings from a non-biblical book? Perhaps you have heard a poem at a carol service, or a popular text such as Henry Scott-Holland's 'Death is nothing at all' read at a funeral. The presence of non-biblical readings in Christian worship raises several questions on which to reflect.

- How have you felt about a non-biblical reading in a service of worship? Or, if you have not had this experience, how do you think you would feel about it?
- What is the status of these non-biblical texts? Does the fact that they are being read in worship mean that we should believe what they say?
- How do we respond if we think that they are not conveying a Christian truth (what if we do not believe, for example, that death is indeed 'nothing at all')?
- Are there limits to what it is appropriate to read in the context of worship? How do we know what these limits are, and who could set them?

The Bible as a library

It is often said that the Bible is not *a* book but a library of books. The fact, though, that we are used to seeing all the contents of the Bible printed in a uniform order, and bound between two covers, can make us overlook the fact that 'the Bible' was made up from physically separate books, and was only brought together into one volume at a fairly late stage. It makes a big difference if your Bible is a single printed volume with universally agreed contents, or if your 'Bible' is a list of separate scrolls or books whose contents may not be agreed on by all Christians. This second situation, the 'Bible' as a disputed list, was in fact the case for the first few centuries of the Church's existence.

📖 **Read Luke 4:16–19.** Here Jesus in the synagogue at Nazareth stands up to read, and the attendant hands to him 'the scroll of the prophet Isaiah'. If we could see the 'Bible' of the synagogue at Nazareth, it would have consisted of a box containing scrolls, and in the case of most books each would have occupied a separate scroll. The possibility for uncertainty about what was in and what was out of such a 'Bible' is evident: different communities might use different collections.

Defining the Old Testament

EXERCISE

Obtain a Roman Catholic translation of the Bible, such as *The (New) Jerusalem Bible*, and a translation in the Protestant tradition, for instance *The (New) Revised Standard Version, Good News Bible* or *New International Version*. Compare the contents list of the Old Testament in the two Bibles. What differences are there in order and in scope?

Do all Christians have the same Old Testament?

If we added a Hebrew Bible to our comparison we would find a third possibility again, distinct from either of the major Christian arrangements. The Hebrew Bible lacks those works which are found in the Apocrypha of the Protestant Bible, and the books which it does have are ordered differently. The Hebrew Scriptures are explicitly arranged into three groupings. First comes the Law (Genesis to Deuteronomy). This is followed by the Prophets, a section which is further subdvided into the Former Prophets (Joshua to 2 Kings) and the Latter Prophets (all the prophetic books of the Protestant canon except Daniel). The third grouping is known as the Writings and contains Psalms, Proverbs, Job, the five *Megilloth* or Scrolls (Song of Songs, Ruth, Lamentations, Ecclesiastes and Esther), Daniel, Ezra, Nehemiah and Chronicles.

The manifest differences between these listings is evidence that the growth of the Old Testament canon is a complex story. The account which will be given here is necessarily brief and simplified.

It should also be noted that what is said here would be contested by some scholars. Further details on the development of the Old Testament canon can be found in: Beckwith, 1985; Beckwith, 1994, pp. 100–102; Brown and Collins, 1989, pp. 1037–1043.

Were the Hebrew Scriptures fixed by New Testament times?

Was the Christian Church born, as one writer has put it, with a Bible in its cradle? Or were the limits of Scripture still unclear at the edges?

The New Testament itself contains some evidence that the scriptural canon of the Jewish community was not entirely fixed, and that there was uncertainty about the status of at least some books, of which a number found their way eventually into the Hebrew canon while others did not. This evidence would include the following observations.

- References to the third section of the Hebrew canon (the Writings) before the late first century AD are vague. Hence, the Preface to Ecclesiasticus (c. 130 BC) mentions 'the Law, the Prophets, and *the writers who followed in their steps*', and Luke seems to refer to this section as 'Psalms' (Luke 24:44). This might suggest a degree of hesitation about the exact limits of this third section of the canon.
- There were debates within Judaism after AD 70 as to whether certain books (notably Song of Songs and Ecclesiastes) were to be regarded as sacred.
- The Dead Sea Scrolls include fragments of all the books of the present Hebrew Old Testament (except Esther – also largely ignored by the New Testament), but they also include fragments of several works now in the Apocrypha (such as Tobit and the Letter of Jeremiah) and some works which were excluded from the apocrypha, and are known as 'pseudepigrapha' (such as Jubilees and 1 Enoch). We cannot know what status was accorded to these books, but the Dead Sea Scrolls show us a first-century Jewish community which read and valued (at the least) a wider collection than the present-day Hebrew canon.
- New Testament authors are quite similar to the writers of the Dead Sea Scrolls in this respect – they include allusions (at least) to several books not in the final Hebrew canon. These include works, such as Ecclesiasticus, which made their way into the Apocrypha of Protestant Bibles (compare Ecclesiasticus 17:26 and 2 Timothy 2:19), and they also include books which were not even accepted into the Apocrypha: in Jude 14 there is a reference to 1 Enoch. Certainly, no New Testament writer directly appeals to these apocryphal or extra-canonical books as Scripture, but allusions to them came readily to the mind of the New Testament writers.

Most scholars conclude on the basis of these pieces of evidence that, at the time at which Christianity arose, the Jewish community had not yet determined completely which books were to be included in their list of sacred writings. It should be noted that this point is disputed by some scholars, who argue that the Hebrew canon was indeed fixed well before the New Testament period (Beckwith, 1985).

The Old Testament: a canon in three stages

The most common understanding today of the development of the Old Testament canon sees it as a gradual process, taking place over many centuries, and giving rise successively to each of the three sections of the Scriptures: Law, Prophets and Writings.

The Law

This appears to have been the first stage of the Hebrew Scriptures to be defined and closed.

Our first solid evidence for the appeal to written texts as an authority for faith and practice (that is as 'Scripture') comes in 2 Kings 22:8 to 23:3. In this important passage, King Josiah of Judah set himself to reform the life of the nation in accordance with the 'book of the Law' which had been found in the Temple (c. 622 BC). The consensus of scholars is that this 'book of the Law' was either Deuteronomy or an earlier draft of Deuteronomy. From this point on, the written Law assumed an increasing importance in the life of the people.

Written Law may have grown in importance particularly during the Exile in Babylon (sixth century BC), when knowledge of the Law and observance of it would have helped ensure the coherence of the Jewish community. After the Exile, the acceptance of the Law was a major part of the reforms of Ezra and Nehemiah (Ezra 7:14; Nehemiah 8:1). By the time Ezra and Nehemiah had completed their reforms (c. 400 BC) the five books of the Law were established as the core and foundation of Israel's Scripture. No other books were admitted to this core after this time, and so we can speak of the first stage of canon formation as being complete by that date.

The Prophets

The words of the prophets, and in some cases their actions too, were noted even in their own times. There is evidence that their words were written down during their lifetimes: Isaiah 8:16 and Jeremiah 36:4 imply that disciples or followers of the prophets preserved the prophets' message. The same followers, of course, may also have reinterpreted the prophets' words and deeds, as time went by, to make them applicable to changed situations.

The section of the Hebrew Bible known as the 'Former Prophets' (Joshua to Kings) seems to have been composed in the exilic period (the last recorded event, 2 Kings 25:27, is the release of King Jehoiachin c. 560 BC) but it clearly depended on earlier sources which have been lost. Many scholars have come to believe that the same group within Judaism which compiled the histories in the 'Former Prophets' also compiled and edited the 'Latter Prophets', and if this is right, it might help explain the connection which the Hebrew canon makes between the two branches of the 'Prophets' section.

The book of Ecclesiasticus (c. 190/180 BC) gives us some indication that the Prophets were regarded as Scripture at the time it was written. In the best-known passage of the book, which begins 'Let us now praise famous men' (Ecclesiasticus 44:1), after detailing the stories of the patriarchs and Moses (the Law: 44:16 to 45:26), the author moves on to extol the heroes of the nation between Joshua and the Exile (the Former Prophets: 46:1 to 49:6). He also summarises the Latter Prophets: Isaiah (48:20–25), Jeremiah (49:6–7), Ezekiel (49:8) and the twelve minor prophets (49:10). By around 200 BC, therefore, we can say on the evidence in Ecclesiasticus that the Former and the Latter Prophets were joined to the Law as part of the Scriptures of Israel.

The Writings

We have already looked at the uncertainty about this section of the Scriptures which seems still to have existed among Jews in New Testament times. About AD 90 the Jewish historian Josephus enumerated the Jewish Scriptures as: five law books, thirteen books of the prophets, and four books which were 'hymns to God and precepts for the conduct of human life' (*Against Apion*, 1.8). This is the first real listing of sacred books which has come down to us, and Josephus' total of twenty-two may be meant to conform to the number of letters in the Hebrew alphabet. About AD 100, the apocryphal work known as 2 Esdras (or 4 Ezra) counted twenty-four books in total, and this has become the traditional Hebrew enumeration. But even after this date some Jews continued to read, and treat as sacred, books such as Ecclesiasticus which are not now in the Hebrew canon. It seems most likely that the canon was not fixed until the late second century AD, at least as far as the Writings are concerned, and that in consequence we must conclude that the early

Christians did not take from Judaism a fixed and definite list of Scriptures. The Church was not born with a clearly defined Old Testament in its cradle.

EXERCISE

📖 **Read 2 Kings 22; Nehemiah 8.**

These passages deal with the effect of reading the Law on national life, first under Josiah (seventh century BC – probably here 'the book of the Law' was Deuteronomy) and then under Ezra (fifth century BC). What do these passages tell us about the esteem in which written traditions of Torah were held in these periods?

The Christian Old Testament canon

The early Church

Right from the beginning of the Church's existence, Christians relied in large measure, not on the Hebrew-language Scriptures, but on the Greek translation of the Old Testament known as the 'Septuagint'. This translation was generally used in Greek-speaking synagogues, and it passed over into the life of the Church. It is today the version of the Old Testament used liturgically by Greek Orthodox Christians.

This Greek Septuagint, though, did not have a fixed content in its early stages. It certainly included a number of books not found in the Hebrew canon. The reason for this more extensive collection has never been convincingly explained. Some scholars have supposed that the longer collection, adopted by the Christians, represents the scriptural collection of the Jews who lived in Alexandria in Egypt, where there was a large and highly educated Greek-speaking Jewish community. The shorter collection, on this view, would represent the canon of the Palestinian Jews. But the manuscripts from the Dead Sea (the so-called 'Dead Sea Scrolls') have now shown us that the Hebrew-speakers who produced the Scrolls also valued works which are found in this wider collection. So it would seem that the longer collection was not a peculiarity of Greek-speaking Jews.

Early Christian biblical manuscripts included these 'extra' books (though not always exactly the same ones), and early Christian writers appealed to them in their arguments. So books such as Maccabees,

Ecclesiasticus and Wisdom gained a revered place in the Church's life –
but their place was never entirely secure. By the end of the second century (at the latest) the Jews had fixed the boundaries of the Hebrew
Scriptures, and Christians found that their own 'extra' books were not
accepted by the Jews. Christian scholars also noticed that the New
Testament itself makes no more than allusions to these 'extra' books.
Some Christians, including the great Bible translator Jerome
(d. 419/20), urged that the Christian canon should be reduced to the
narrower collection of the Hebrew Scriptures. But the custom of reading and using the 'extra' books in the Church was too strong, and the
medieval Church, in consequence, found itself with a two-tier Old
Testament canon: the narrower collection became known as the
'protocanonical' works (those of the 'first canon'), and the extra books
became known as the 'deuterocanonical' works (those of the 'second
canon').

The Reformation and after

The Reformation of the sixteenth century brought about a rethinking of
the Old Testament canon. The Protestant Churches decided to follow
the policy which Jerome had advocated long before, and removed the
deuterocanonical works from their Old Testament. To the arguments
used in the early Church was added a new one: these deuterocanonical
works included proof texts for doctrines of which the Reformers disapproved (particularly purgatory in 2 Maccabees 12:45). The Reformers
placed these excluded works in a kind of appendix to the Old Testament, the 'Apocrypha' (which strictly should mean 'hidden things').

The Church of England appealed to Jerome's opinion to make its case
that 'the other books (as *Hierome* saith) the Church doth read for example of life and instruction in manners [i.e. conduct]; but yet doth it not
apply them to establish any doctrine' (Article 6). Other Churches of the
Reformation took a more severe view and removed the Apocrypha altogether, and the Westminster Confession of 1648, which gave expression
to English Puritanism, stated: 'The books commonly called Apocrypha,
not being of divine inspiration, are not part of the canon of Scripture;
and therefore of no authority to the Church of God, not to be otherwise
approved, or made use of, than other human writings.' In 1827 the
British and Foreign Bible Society decided to omit the Apocrypha from
printings of the Bible, and from that time it became normal to find
English-language Bibles without the Apocrypha.

The Roman Catholic Church, despite some misgivings, recognised the longer canon at the Council of Trent (*De Canonicis Scripturis*, 4th Session, 1546).

The apparently simple differences in the contents pages of Roman Catholic and Protestant Bibles turn out to be the result of complex historical developments, about which our sources do not always give us very full information.

Questioning the notion of 'canon'

In this chapter it has been assumed that having a canon of the Old Testament is a good thing, and the emergence of the canon was a clear historical process, ending up with a list of canonical Scriptures.

P R Davies (1998), though, has argued for a very different picture of the process of Old Testament canonisation. He has made a number of criticisms of the traditional understanding of canon-formation.

- There was no single trajectory moving inevitably towards the creation of a single Old Testament canon. There were always (at least as long as Israel had anything which could be called 'Scripture') various canons in the process of formation. So we should not be surprised by the variations in canonical listing between Jews, Protestants and Catholics: the canon has always been fluid.
- Canonisation is an exercise in power. In the ancient world, the production of a canon of 'official' writings represented the imposition of a set of values on a community by a literary and political elite – in this case, the Jewish scribal groups whose views came to dominate in Judaism of the first and second centuries of the Christian era.
- Davies takes a negative view of the creation of canons. While the *process* of canonisation is a testimony to living debate and struggle within a religious community, the *imposition* of a canon represents the opposite of such a living process: 'While canonizing does entail listing, organising, and labeling, a single definitive list is not, indeed, the *purpose* of the canonizing process, any more than death is the purpose of life: merely its end' (Davies, 1998, p. 58).

EXERCISE
Why do we need a canon of Scripture? Should we be prepared to have an open-ended list of sacred writings? What criteria could govern such a list? Could a devotionally useful book (C S Lewis' *Screwtape Letters*, for instance) be accepted as Scripture? ▶▶

Davies' description of canonisation is essentially cultural and historical, and could apply to any community (political or academic, as well as religious). Is there any *theological* criterion which distinguishes canonical Scripture for the Christian Church, and means that it has to be closed at some point (for instance, to qualify as Scripture, a writing must be near to the key events to which the community of faith looks as constitutive)?

Further reading

Beckwith, R T (1985), *The Old Testament Canon of the New Testament Church*, Grand Rapids, Michigan, Eerdmans.

Beckwith, R T (1993), Canon of the Hebrew Bible and the Old Testament, in B M Metzger and M D Coogan (eds), *The Oxford Companion to the Bible*, pp. 100–102, Oxford, Oxford University Press.

Brown, R E and Collins, R (1989), Canonicity, in R E Brown et al. (eds), *The New Jerome Biblical Commentary*, pp. 1034–1054, London, Geoffrey Chapman.

Davies, P R (1998), *Scribes and Schools: the canonization of the Hebrew Scriptures*, London, SPCK.

Sundberg, A C (1964), *The Old Testament of the Early Church*, Cambridge, Massachusetts, Harvard University Press.

7. DEFINING THE NEW TESTAMENT

Introduction

There is no substantial disagreement among the major Churches about the extent of the New Testament canon as there is about the Old, but the canon of the New Testament still raises historical and theological problems.

📖 **Read 2 Timothy 3:16.** Why do we need a New Testament? Some people might say the New Testament is there in order to provide us with information on Jesus and the early Christians. In the following extract, John Barton suggests that our own experience tells us that we do not in fact commonly use the New Testament in this way, and that the way we do use it is more in conformity with the thrust of 2 Timothy 3:16.

> The earlier generations of Christians who held what might look like a 'high' fundamentalist view of the Bible . . . saw the Bible as a 'training in righteousness', as 2 Timothy 3:16 puts it. And modern evangelicals really have much the same thing in mind. A Bible-study group is not designed to inform, at least not in the usual sense of the word, but to 'form' the Christians who attend it in the mould of Christian life and obedience which God intends. (Barton, 1997a, p. 148)

Reflecting on experience

Does this quotation from Barton describe your experience of the Bible? Do we use the New Testament to mould our lives *rather than* to gain information? Or is Barton too dismissive of the information-giving role of the New Testament?

The emergence of Christian Scripture

It was by no means obvious that Christians would produce and accept a second collection of writings to stand alongside their initial Scriptures (that is the Old Testament). After all, everything which the New Testament writers stated about the sufficiency of the Scriptures (2 Timothy 3:15–16), or concerning their authority (John 10:35), or describing their witness to Christ (Luke 24:44), or commending their relevance to Christian living (1 Corinthians 10:11) referred to the *Old* Testament, and not to the New which did not yet exist. (The only exceptions to this could be 1 Timothy 5:18 and 2 Peter 3:16 which *may* place a gospel writing and Paul's letters respectively on a level with the Old Testament.) A candid reading of the New Testament suggests that the first generations of Christians were content with the Old Testament as their Scripture. In it they found the proofs of Christ's messiahship, his saving death and life-giving resurrection. From it they drew the moral guidance which they needed. All that they preached, lived, argued and wrote, they did without having a New Testament alongside the Old.

In the previous chapter, we noted the fact that the Jewish community preserved its Scriptures as a collection of scrolls, and that from this aspect of book production sprang the potential for differences about the exact extent of the canon of Scripture. Even though the early Christians made the transition for their Scriptures from the scroll to the modern style of book (known as the *codex*) at an early stage, they were in a similar situation to the Jewish community in that they kept their Scripture in separate books for a long time. In AD 180 a group of Christians was arrested in a North African town called Scilli, and eventually martyred. Part of their interrogation concerned their Scriptures. 'What is in your book-box?' they were asked. 'Books', they replied, 'and the letters of Paul, a good man.' As in the synagogue a century and a half previously, their 'Bible' consisted of what was in their book-box. If a Church kept edifying literature in its book-box, did that make it 'Scripture'? There was plenty of scope for uncertainty at this stage about what was and what was not 'Scripture'.

We have to imagine, then, the first Christians gathering together the books which now make up our New Testament, and we must suppose that this process was spread over the course of time. We have to discover why they felt that they needed a New Testament to stand alongside their existing Scriptures, and how they set about gathering and defining this new collection.

EXERCISE
📖 **Read Acts 15:1–21.**

This passage reports an important decision of the early Christians at the so-called 'Council of Jerusalem' on the subject of admitting Gentiles into the Church: did Gentiles need to be circumcised, and should they keep the Law of the Old Testament in its entirety or in part? The outcome of the Council was a decision that Gentiles should observe a minimum of ritual laws which would enable table fellowship with Jewish believers to continue.

For our purposes, the important thing is the nature of the arguments brought forward. Identify which of the following the participants appealed to in their arguments:
• Old Testament Scriptures;
• Christian writings;
• the example of Jesus;
• apostolic experience.

In the light of what you have found in this passage, where would you say that the first Christians looked for authoritative guidance?

Words of the apostles: the start of Christian Scripture

You will have noticed in thinking over Acts 15:1–21 that the main appeal was to the experience of the apostles (Peter vv. 6–11, 14; Paul and Barnabas v. 12), supported by texts of Scripture (vv. 16–18, from Jeremiah 12:15 and Amos 9:11–12). The early Christians were convinced that the Old Testament prophesied what was now happening in their experience, the coming of the Christ and the opening of salvation to the Gentiles. In other words, Christian experience, and especially the teaching and example of the apostles, was the key to unlock the true meaning of the Old Testament.

The first Christians might have done what other Jewish groups of the time did, and expressed their new ideas by producing commentaries and rewritings of the Old Testament. This was the way, for instance, in which the people who wrote the Dead Sea Scrolls operated. But instead, the first Christians produced a body of writing which took its origin in the life and ministry of Jesus and in the experience and teaching of the Church itself – in other words, the gospels and letters of our New Testament.

Jesus had laid the foundations for this approach. Although he frequently referred to the Scriptures, his teaching was not developed around scriptural commentary or exegesis, and this was a departure from the typical style of the rabbis of his day. Jesus normally set before his hearers something new from his own example and teaching (Mark 1:22). So it was in conformity with what Jesus had done that, as with the Council of Jerusalem, Christians took the experience and teaching of their leaders, apostles in particular, as their guide in living their Christian lives (1 Corinthians 11:1; Philippians 3:17; 4:9; 1 Thessalonians 1:5–6; Hebrews 13:7).

This authoritative and normative teaching of the apostles was available to the Churches through writings, and especially letters. Paul wrote with instruction and advice to the Churches he had founded, and in at least one case (Romans) to a Church he had not founded. He wrote as an 'apostle to the Gentiles' (Romans 11:13), and he wrote with an authority which looked for respect and even demanded obedience. His letters, so to speak, projected his presence into the Churches: Paul considered that he was (at least potentially) 'present in the spirit' with his Churches (1 Corinthians 5:3–4), and his letters actualised that presence by making his very words available to the Church to which he wrote. Some people even thought he came across better in his letters than when he was physically present (2 Corinthians 10:10).

It is clear that Paul's letters were read, noted and discussed right from the start. What is probably Paul's earliest surviving letter contains an instruction that it should be read to the whole Church (1 Thessalonians 5:27). A letter from Paul could overawe and even frighten a Church which received it (2 Corinthians 10:1, 9). The weight which Paul's letters carried was so great that people were soon writing false letters in his name to cash in on his authority (2 Thessalonians 2:2). Perhaps as a result of this, Paul seems to have taken to writing a short postscript in his own characteristic handwriting to authenticate his letters (2 Thessalonians 3:17 – some scholars doubt the authenticity of 2 Thessalonians, but there is a similar postscript in 1 Corinthians, Galatians, Colossians and Philemon).

It was not only Paul, of course, who wrote letters. We have already looked at the letter which emanated from the apostolic meeting in Jerusalem (Acts 15:23–29). Our New Testament contains letters written by or in the name of Peter, James, John and Jude, as well as the anonymous Letter to the Hebrews. Revelation, too, seems to have been treated like a letter, and was read to the congregations to which it was addressed (Revelation 1:3; 22:18).

The treasuring of apostolic letters

Christian leaders continued to write letters in the period after the apostles, but those which were believed to come from apostles had from the beginning an authority which distinguished them from later productions, or from purely ephemeral writings of the apostolic era such as the letter of recommendation which the Church in Ephesus wrote for Apollos to take to Achaia (Acts 18:27). 2 Peter 3:16, for instance, shows that Paul's letters were the subject of earnest discussion at an early time (even if, as most scholars conclude, Peter himself did not write this letter).

Letters from apostles or purporting to come from them were passed from Church to Church: Colossians 4:16 refers to the swapping of Pauline letters between Churches. In this way apostolic letters were kept, re-read and studied by the earliest Christians. 2 Peter 3:16 suggests that the writer knew of at least three letters of Paul ('*all* his letters'). We have also the witness of a letter written by Clement, Bishop of Rome, to Corinth towards the end of the first century, and known as *1 Clement*. This letter appeals to the Corinthians to 'Take up the letter of the blessed Paul the Apostle' (1 Clement 47:1), referring to 1 Corinthians. Paul's Corinthian letter was evidently known both to Clement in Rome as well as to the Church in Corinth. Its teaching was a court of appeal for post-apostolic leaders such as Clement. Similarly Ignatius and Polycarp, writing in the early second century to the Ephesians and Philippians respectively, refer their readers to Paul's letters (Ignatius, *Ephesians* 12:2; Polycarp, *Philippians* 3:2). We have already seen how the Church at Scilli in AD 180 had a special place for Paul's letters in its book collection. Apostolic letters were the foundation on which Christian Scripture was built.

EXERCISE

📖 **Read 2 Corinthians 10:1, 9; 2 Thessalonians 2:2; 2 Peter 3:16.**

What different reactions to Paul's letters are described here? Why do you think Paul had the capacity to provoke these responses? Does he still provoke similar responses today?

Witness to Jesus: from word of mouth to written Scripture

It might seem the wrong way round to begin an account of the growth of the New Testament with the letters and not with the gospels, with the words of the apostles and not with the witness to Jesus, but it is in fact much easier to document the impact of the letters on the Churches than that of the gospels.

Good news by word of mouth

It is a near-universal assumption among scholars that the stories and sayings of Jesus were first preserved orally by his followers, and only committed to writing at a rather late stage, say between the mid-sixties and the nineties. This means that all of Paul's letters would have pre-dated the earliest of the gospels (probably Mark). The letters came first, therefore, in point of time.

During this period in which the tradition about Jesus was kept orally by the Church we do not find it being called on very often by the first Christians. It is one of the odd features of Paul's letters, which has puzzled scholars for many years, that Paul seldom refers to the teaching or life of Jesus. But he does make such an appeal sometimes, and when Paul writes, as he does in 1 Corinthians 7:10, 12, 25, about his own advice and contrasts it with 'instruction from the Lord', we should probably assume (as most scholars do) that he is writing about a saying of Jesus. He significantly puts the Lord's instructions alongside the instruction of the Torah (1 Corinthians 9:13–14). Similarly, he had teaching about the End which is not his own but a 'word of the Lord' (1 Thessalonians 4:15). He was also, very significantly, aware of traditions about the Last Supper (1 Corinthians 11:23–26) and the resurrection (1 Corinthians 15:3–7). So, although Paul does not refer often to the teaching of Jesus or to his life, when he does so, Jesus' teaching has an overruling authority.

Good news in writing

For several decades the stories and sayings of Jesus were preserved only, it would seem, in oral form. Since none of the gospel writers dated their work, and no contemporary mentioned the committing of the Jesus-tradition to writing, we cannot be at all sure when our gospels were written. The general view of scholars today is that Mark was the first to be written in the sixties of the first century, followed by Matthew and Luke, with John the latest to be written, in the nineties. As to the motives for writing a gospel, we have only the evidence of the texts themselves to go on, and scholars (as may be imagined) hold many different views. All we can say for certain is that the gospel writers were compelled by their circumstances to make the sayings and deeds of Jesus more widely known. Although we can conjecture what those circumstances might have been (such as the death of the generation which had known Jesus), we cannot be entirely sure exactly what prompted the writing-down of the Jesus-tradition.

The growing importance of the gospels

Even after the gospels were written down, Christians regularly referred to Jesus' words quite loosely, for instance combining sayings from different gospels or paraphrasing his words. This may well indicate that they were still relying on oral traditions rather than referring to the texts of the gospels as we have them today. There is every reason to suppose that well into the second century they continued to value stories and sayings passed on by word of mouth, especially those which could be traced to apostles and their followers. An early Christian named Papias, who lived in the early second century, has left an indication of this kind of attitude in a fragment of his writings which has survived. Describing his quest for real information about Jesus, he wrote how he would seek out people who could tell him at first hand what the apostles had said, 'For I did not suppose that information from books would help me so much as the word of a living and abiding voice' (Papias in Eusebius, *Ecclesiastical History*, 3.39.3–4).

There is no reason to suppose that the gospels were originally written to supercede this word-of-mouth passing-on of the Gospel story. But inevitably, as time passed it became more difficult to find first-hand information, and written gospels began to assume a growing importance. So it is not at all surprising that the first references to *written* gospels do not appear until the second quarter of the second century. Nor is it surprising that from then onwards the gospels acquired a growing importance in the Church: by the 150s we hear of them being read regularly in Christian worship (Justin Martyr, *I Apology* 66), and around AD 185 the Church's first great theologian, Irenaeus, was making great use of all four canonical gospels in his major work *Against Heresies*.

What sort of Scripture?

Four gospels

The emergence of the four gospels as the centrepiece of the New Testament is a vital chapter in the Christian story, but hard to document clearly, and scholarly opinion is divided on how it happened. Some would argue that the four-gospel canon was already well-established by the start of the second century. Others maintain that Christians were content with largely oral tradition about Jesus until the growth of heresies made the Church prize the four gospels as their anchor in the apostolic witness to Jesus. This was particularly important since several heretical groups in the second century claimed that they had *secret* oral traditions: publicly available written records of Jesus were of crucial significance for refuting these claims to a secret tradition.

One challenge to the collection of four gospels was the proposal of Marcion in the mid-second century only to recognise one gospel, which was an edited form of Luke (see Chapter 8). At the same time, some Christians were still writing 'new' gospels, such as the 'Gospel of Peter' and the 'Gospel of Thomas' (Stanton, 1997, pp. 77–95). Should Christians accept or reject these writings?

In addition to these problems of contemporary creativity, there was a strong feeling in some parts of the Church in the second century that the existence of four gospels with rather diverse details was giving support to the Church's critics. Would it not be sensible to produce a single 'harmony' out of the four gospels, so that there would be just one gospel, free from dangerous discrepancies in its narrative? Such a gospel was produced in the late second century by a Syrian called Tatian, and his book (the *Diatessaron*) enjoyed considerable favour for many years (Metzger, 1987, pp. 10–36).

Defining the new Scripture

All of the attempts to improve on the writings which had come from the earliest years of Christianity – Marcion's works, Tatian's *Diatessaron*, the Gospels of Peter and Thomas, and so on – were eventually rejected by the Church. It may be that some second-century writings were unwittingly accepted: if 2 Peter, for instance, was in fact written at a very late stage, as many scholars believe, it could be a product of the second rather than the first century. But if any writings accepted into the Christian Scriptures were indeed written as late as the second century, they were nonetheless accepted because Christians *believed* them to come from the apostolic era.

It is far from clear exactly what criteria were applied to decide what should and what should not be received as Christian Scripture of the new covenant, as our 'New Testament'. Widespread use appears to have been one criterion, and orthodox teaching another. But it seems to have been vital that these Scriptures came from the apostolic times and from the apostolic circle, even if not always (as with Mark or Luke) from apostles themselves. By the end of the second century, if not before, the experience of dealing with Marcion, Tatian and others convinced the majority of Christians that the inheritance of apostolic writings was simply to be received, not to be either improved or supplemented. At some point before AD 190 a priest in Asia (modern Turkey) wrote a book called 'The Acts of Paul' – with the best of motives – inventing a colourful pageant of new episodes in the apostle's life. This 'Acts of Paul' gained a wide readership, but when the authorship became known the book was rejected (Tertullian, *On Baptism* 17, on the internet at: http:www.ccel.org/fathers/). The point was clear, that even edifying and widely read books could not be accepted if they could be shown not to come from the apostolic age.

Equality with the Old Testament?

John Barton has argued in an original line of interpretation that there was what he has called a 'disequilibrium' between the Old and the New Testaments in the early Church. They were not simply regarded in the same light, and Marcion, in attempting to remove the Old Testament altogether, was not acting counter to existing Christian attitudes but was simply exaggerating them. The earliest Christians believed that the Old Testament was 'Scripture', with all the authority which the ancient mind accorded to old literature, but it was eclipsed in *importance* for them by the new records of what God had done in Christ, that is the writings of what later became the New Testament. However, the New Testament could not be 'Scripture' precisely because it was new – it was not 'old enough to have a natural aura of sacred antiquity':

The first Christians had books about Jesus and his first disciples, and they used them as authoritative sources of information about the central events of salvation. These events dwarfed, in their minds, anything in the holy books they had taken over from Judaism. But they did not yet regard the written records of these events as 'ancient scriptures' in the same sense as the 'Old Testament' . . . These books were more important than 'Scripture'. (Barton, 1997b, pp. 67–68)

In Barton's view, the earliest Christianity was novel and distinctive precisely because it believed that what God was doing in the present was more important than what he had done in the past. However, this distinctiveness could not be maintained, and Christianity soon turned into something more like a normal religion of the ancient world. The authentic early Christian view was already being lost by the time that the Pastoral Epistles and 2 Peter were written (presumably well into the second century), because we find them 'respecting the authorities of the past rather than the freshness of the present'. Paradoxically, treating the New Testament in the same way as the Old was not a promotion but a diminution of the New Testament. It showed that Christianity had lost its sense of 'God's fresh activity' and had replaced it with 'that reverence for the past which was the hallmark of the ancient religious mind' (Barton, 1997b, p. 68).

Barton locates the authentic Christian attitude in the earliest phase of the Church, and argues that this authentic 'fresh' attitude was soon overlaid by a more stereotypical religious outlook. Barton's is in its essential elements a very Protestant argument: the dead hand of 'early Catholicism' soon (on this view) squeezed the life and originality from the Church's existence.

EXERCISE
One writer (G Widengren, cited in Evans, 1971, p. 6) described the writing-down of the oral tradition about Jesus as 'a sign of a loss of nerve'. He meant that the Church would have done better with a flexible, evolving tradition about Jesus, rather than a fixed written set of gospels. This is rather similar to Davies' criticism of the Old Testament canon, which we examined in the previous chapter. Was Widengren right? What would we lose if we did not have gospels written in the first century?

The canon today

After the Christian Church had come to recognise that it had *some* scriptures which were of an equal, or even greater, authority than the Old Testament, it still had not decided *which* scriptures these were. Discussions on the extent of the canon were long-lasting: the first listing of New Testament books which exactly agrees with the content of our 27 book New Testament only occurs in 367 (Thirty-Ninth Festal Letter of Athanasius), and doubts about the second and third letters of John and about Revelation were not finally settled for several centuries.

Towards the start of this chapter, we posed the question of whether the Church created the canon of the Scripture. This chapter has attempted to give some reasons for supposing that the Church in fact *recognised* the qualities of the works which are now found in our Bibles. B M Metzger, in his book on the canon of the New Testament, put the issue in this way:

> During the second and succeeding centuries, this authoritative word [of God] was found, not in the utterances of contemporary leaders and teachers, but in the apostolic testimony contained within certain early Christian writings. From this point of view the Church did not create the canon, but came to recognize, accept, affirm and confirm the self-authenticating quality of certain documents that imposed themselves as such upon the Church. If this fact is obscured, one comes into serious conflict not with dogma but with history. (Metzger, 1987, p. 287)

EXERCISE

Many people find that Christian classics, great and small, 'speak' to them – it is not just the Bible. One might think of examples such as C S Lewis' *Screwtape Letters* or *Narnia Chronicles*. John Bunyan, in his autobiographical work *Grace Abounding to the Chief of Sinners*, describes how a text came into his mind during a time of great perplexity which gave him comfort, and which he assumed was from the (Protestant) Bible. He was astonished not to be able to find it from one end of the Bible to the other – and even more surprised some time later when a friend told him it came from the Apocrypha, which he did not believe was inspired at all! ▶▶

- Have you ever found a non-biblical text 'speak' to you in this way?
- How are such texts related to the Bible?
- What sort of inspiration (if any) do you think they have?

Further reading

Barton, J (1997), *What is the Bible?* London, SPCK (second edition).

Barton, J (1997), *The Spirit and the Letter: studies in the biblical canon*, London, SPCK.

Evans, C (1971), *Is 'Holy Scripture' Christian? and other questions*, London, SCM.

Metzger, B M (1987), *The Canon of the New Testament*, Oxford, Oxford University Press.

Patzia, A G (1995), *The Making of the New Testament: origin, collection, canon*, Downers Grove, Illinois, Inter Varsity and Leicester, Apollos.

Stanton, G (1997), *Gospel Truth? today's quest for Jesus of Nazareth*, London, HarperCollins (second edition).

8. THE OLD TESTAMENT AND THE CHRISTIAN BIBLE

Introduction

It is a frequent complaint that the Old Testament is neglected in sermons and overlooked by Christian readers of the Scriptures. In the Anglican Prayer Book of 1662 a reading from the Old Testament was prescribed for Morning and Evening Prayer alongside the New and was accompanied by Psalms, but Old Testament readings appeared only very rarely at the service of Holy Communion. The Second Vatican Council lamented the neglect of the Old Testament by Roman Catholics and urged closer study of it (*Dei Verbum*, 1965, chapter 4).

Partly in response to Vatican II, modern lectionaries, which are often ecumenical, now include far more material from the Old Testament within the Eucharist. More encouragement is being given for congregations to listen to the Old Testament, but it is still likely to be the case that if a reading is omitted, it will be the one from the Old Testament, and the complaint about the scarcity of preaching from the Old Testament also remains.

Reflecting on experience
Is it the case that Christian readers neglect the Old Testament? How frequently, in your experience, are sermons based on Old Testament passages?

If it is the case that Christian reading and preaching favours the New over the Old, can you think of any reasons why this may be? Here are some suggestions which you might want to furnish with examples. You may be able to think of other reasons: ▶▶

- obscurity – the Old Testament can be difficult to understand;
- irrelevance – all those laws do not apply to Christians;
- harshness – there is too much about law and judgement, and not enough about love and mercy;
- incompleteness – it does not say anything about Christ.

Christian reading of the Old Testament

We have already seen in previous chapters that the first Christians read the Old Testament assiduously. It was their Bible. The difference between then and now is, partly, that we have a New Testament and so we are open to the temptation to give an overwhelming priority to this New Testament, which speaks directly about Christ, over the Old, which does not. As Elizabeth Achtemeier has put it: 'the average layperson in the pew and even many preachers still regard the Old Testament as an unnecessary prelude to the "real" New Testament Bible' (Achtemeier, 1995, p. 124).

There are numerous books dealing with the ways in which the Old Testament can be read as Christian Scripture. The Old Testament can be read as the necessary historical background for the coming of Christ, or as theological preparation for the Christian Gospel, or (in the way Luther did) as setting out the Law which will convince people of their need for the Gospel. Useful books dealing with these sort of questions include: Baker, 1976; Barr, 1982; Barton, 1984; Goldingay 1990, 1995.

We do not have the space to deal with all of these issues in this chapter, and we will in consequence be concentrating on one main issue: Does the Old Testament belong in the Christian Bible on an equal footing with the New?

In the opening exercise 'Reflecting on experience', we considered a widespread sense that the Old Testament is not always placed on an equal footing with the New, and thought of some reasons why this might be. We have now to ask whether this widespread demotion of the Old Testament is right and proper, or whether it is something to be regretted and countered. We begin this investigation by considering the first and most radical challenge posed to the Old Testament as Christian Scripture, that of Marcion.

The Old Testament: Marcion's radical solution

One of the greatest controversies which the Church faced in the second century was caused by a wealthy shipping magnate, who moved from his home in what is now Turkey to Rome in the 140s. This man, Marcion, used his wealth to propogate his innovative and radical ideas about Christianity – although in the end even his lavish spending could not convince the Church that he was right, and in AD 144 he was excommunicated. His response was to set up his own church, which attracted enough followers to be a genuine problem for the majority Church over the subsequent decades.

Marcion wanted to abandon the Old Testament altogether and con-struct a new scripture based on the letters of Paul and the Gospel of Luke. His ideas seem to disclose an implicit anti-Semitism of a sort which has surfaced in the Church on many occasions since his day. But the ostensible basis of his bold restructuring of Christian Scripture was a theological one. Such was the reaction against Marcion in the Church that all copies of his books have been lost – presumably orthodox Chris-tians considered it too dangerous to allow their preservation. But from statements in works written to refute him, we know that he believed the following propositions which, taken together, justified his plan.

1. The god revealed in the Old Testament is not the supreme God, but an inferior deity who made this world and who, as 'the god of this world', is in fact the enemy of the supreme God.

2. The inferiority of this creator god of the Old Testament is shown, for instance, by his ignorance of Adam's whereabouts in the Garden of Eden (Genesis 3:9), and his ethical failings are clear when we consi-der the vengeful 'eye for an eye' morality which he demanded. The Jews had been deluded into serving this inferior god, and the Old Testament is his revelation.

3. Far from being a continuation of the revelation of this creator god, Christ's coming was a revelation of the supreme God. His task was to unmask the truth about the inferior creator god, to bring a higher morality ('turn the other cheek' instead of 'an eye for an eye'), and to lead those who accepted his message to salvation from out of the clutches of the 'god of this world'.

4. Unfortunately, the mission of Christ had been obscured by those who should have been proclaiming it. Most of the early (Jewish) leadership of the Church had been unable to break free from thraldom to the inferior god. Only Paul had really understood what

Jesus had been about, hence his conflicts with other leaders such as James and Peter. So, Paul's letters (or a suitable selection from them) formed one section of Marcion's new scripture. The other section was made up of the Gospel of Luke, favoured for reasons obscure to us, but perhaps because of Luke's companionship with Paul. However, even Luke needed editing, as some regrettably 'Jewish' passages had crept in: Marcion, for example, cut out the whole birth narrative in Luke, the account of John the Baptist, and the genealogy of Jesus. In this way he could produce a scripture which conveyed what he thought was the true, original message of Jesus.

Marcion's new scripture has a great importance in the history of the canon: he seems to have been the first Christian to draw up a list of what was, and by implication what was *not*, Christian Scripture. It is probable that his provocative move stimulated the main body of the Church to define its own canon more clearly.

If Marcion had succeeded, the Christian Church would have developed very differently from the way it has done. In one respect, Marcion raised questions about the *canon*: how do we define what is Christian Scripture? In another, he raised questions about the *authority* of what we would now call the New Testament: do we understand Christ better than the New Testament witness and so can we correct what the New Testament writers say? He raised questions about *God*: is the Father of Jesus Christ also creator of the world? But for our purposes the most significant questions Marcion raised were to do with the *Old Testament*: although these books were written before Christ came, are they nonetheless Christian Scripture?

Second-century Christians rejected Marcion because they wanted to adhere to the whole witness of the Scriptures, not merely to pick out elements from which they could construct their own ideas. And had not Jesus himself used the Old Testament Scriptures to show that his coming was foreseen (Luke 24:27, 44–47)?

In response to Marcion, mainstream Christians settled the issue of whether the Old Testament Scriptures belonged in the Christian Bible – they did. It is, as E Achtemeier has pointed out, legitimate for Christians to refer to it as the Old Testament of the Church and not just as the Hebrew Scriptures (Achtemeier, 1995, pp. 125–126). However, once we have settled that the Old Testament is the Scripture of the Church, the Church has to deal with the further problems of how to 'baptise' these writings from *before* the coming of Christ. Marcion had put his finger on some issues which would never entirely go away.

EXERCISE

What would a Christian Church without the Old Testament be like? How would Christian attitudes be different on (for instance) the following topics:

- creation, and humanity's place within it;
- ethics and social justice;
- the Jewish community and the faith of Judaism?

The medieval solution

Christian readers were quite aware that the Old Testament taken in its plain sense could yield a meaning which might be hard to reconcile with the New. To take one example, the wholehearted support for Israel in its warfare with its neighbours is a prominent feature of the historical books and might not seem appropriate for Christians. Indeed, when Bishop Ulfilas prepared a Bible translation for the newly converted Goths about AD 360, 'he prudently suppressed the four books of Kings [1Samuel to 2 Kings], as they might tend to irritate the fierce and sanguinary spirit of the Barbarians' (Gibbon, 1776/88, chapter 37). St Benedict's *Rule* for monks similarly forbade reading anything from the books of Kings in the evening, as they might prove too exciting for the brethren before bedtime!

The Christian answer was not to take the Old Testament in its plain sense, or at any rate to suppose that the plain sense was the least important aspect of the text. We have already looked at the use of allegorical exegesis by Origen in the third century. The process which he pioneered, of seeking a 'spiritual' sense in the Scriptures, was rapidly and widely adapted. It could be seen as no more than an extension of the interpretative pattern we find in the New Testament, such as Paul's statement of principle that the narratives of the Old Testament happened 'as warnings to us' (1 Corinthians 10:6) and had a significance which was 'symbolic' (1 Corinthians 10:11).

In sensitive hands, the quest for the 'spiritual' sense did not entirely lose sight of the historical or 'literal' meaning. While some interpreters followed Origen's radical suggestion that there were passages in the Old Testament which were simply absurd or immoral and could therefore only be understood in a figurative sense, most believed that the Old Testament in its literal sense was historically 'true' (that is, relating events which actually happened). This literal sense had some use in teaching simple people, although the real scholar would want to move on to the more demanding quest for the spiritual sense.

However, when the Fathers came across passages which seemed unedifying, they still tended to argue that the spiritual sense took the place of the historical. So, for instance, when St Jerome had to confront the story in 1 Kings 1:1–4 of how the courtiers of the dying King David brought to his bed a beautiful virgin in the hope of reviving him, this great Bible scholar and ascetic could only interpret this as an image or figurative way of speaking about the *wisdom* which David sought. The Song of Songs, of course, had to be interpreted in its entirety in this 'spiritual' sense.

The Old Testament as Christian Scripture today

EXERCISE

📖 **Read Joshua 10.**

There are a number of important questions to raise from this passage, but for our purposes, we shall concentrate on one: does a passage such as Joshua 10 speak to us of the Christian God, or not?

- If it *does*, then how do we reconcile (on the one hand) the commands in this text to engage in utterly merciless ethnic cleansing, with (on the other) belief in the God revealed by Jesus?
- And if it does *not*, what is this passage doing in the Christian Bible?

The medieval 'spiritual' reading of the Old Testament was a way (amongst other things) of finding an edifying and suitable meaning in a biblical passage such as this violent chapter from Joshua. The medievals could 'spiritualise' the details, and if necessary ignore the literal sense. But if we think that their method of finding a meaning in the text was too much like the way in which a conjuror 'finds' a rabbit in his hat because he has already put it there before he begins, then we have to discover some alternative way of making sense of the difficult passages which (after all) had provided Marcion with some of his ammunition.

The following are some suggestions of ways in which modern readers might make sense of the Old Testament as Christian Scripture today.

Development

It might be argued that the conception of 'holy war' in Joshua belongs to a primitive stage in the development of God's people which has long ago been left behind and is surpassed by the revelation of the New Testament. This approach might be a way of saying implicitly that Joshua 10 does not (or at least not in all respects) speak to us of the Christian God. This view has the merit of taking seriously the process of historical development within Israel, and could be consistent with the traditional Christian understanding of progressive revelation. On the other hand, the peril of this 'developmental' view has been well summarised by E Achtemeier:

> The Church as a whole lost the Old Testament somewhere between 1875 and 1933, when developmentalism was the fashion. The Old Testament was, it came to be thought, simply the record of the natural evolutionary development of ideas and institutions, from their lowest form to their highest, beginning with the prophetic faith and proceeding to the New Testament, with the teachings of Jesus representing the highest peak of the development. (Achtemeier, 1995, p. 123)

Accommodation

Alternatively, it might be accepted that the 'holy war' tradition (with all its unacceptable features) was part of God's self-revelation which *had* to accommodate itself to the culture of its times. How else can God communicate but through the thought-forms of people in their particular historical setting?

This tenth chapter of Joshua also contains the statement that the sun stood still in the sky for Joshua and his men. As early as the time of Galileo in the seventeenth century, interpreters who had accepted the heliocentric theory of the universe were arguing that the Scripture accommodated its expressions to the prevailing assumptions of its own time (see Chapter 4), so the assumption in Joshua 10 that the sun moves while the earth stands still is not to be taken as an *assertion* that the sun moves around the earth, but is merely part of the cultural assumptions of the time.

Something similar might be said about the warfare of the Old Testament: Scripture necessarily has to be couched in the terms of its originating culture, otherwise it could not have arisen in the first place. Our task is to discern an enduring message in what is being *affirmed* and distinguish it from the thought-forms which are merely being *assumed*. There are bound to be differences of opinion in this area. As we saw when we examined the Bible and science, some Christians today believe that the Bible affirms the special creation of humanity, while others believe that the language of Genesis 1 is using the assumptions of an ancient culture to affirm a message about humanity's status. There might be similar disagreements about what is being *affirmed* about God and what is merely being *assumed* in a passage such as Joshua 10. The attempt to use the concept of accommodation to understand Joshua 10 as Christian Scripture will therefore inevitably entail rather subjective decisions: some interpreters might want to hold on to the theological ideas in the Old Testament, while others would feel compelled to jettison many of these ideas as really nothing more than cultural 'baggage'.

Here, for example, is one writer who sets the 'holy war' tradition of Joshua in its cultural context, and argues that it may have been necessary in its time but that we must 'disown' these parts of the Bible:

> Historically, we can try to understand the extreme intolerance of early Israelite religion and its drive to wage a holy war on the practitioners of the heathen religion of Canaan. We could say that it was a necessary stage on the route to the pure monotheism that now characterises Judaism, Christianity, and Islam. Monotheism can *survive* without intolerance . . . But maybe it would never have *arisen* except out of a religious tradition that had passed through an aggressively intolerant phase. (Barton, 1997a, p. 105)

EXERCISE
📖 **Read Exodus 21:22–25 and Matthew 5:38–42.**

Does the 'accommodation' approach to reading the Old Testament as Christian Scripture help us make sense of the relationship between these two passages?

Theological critique

The next approach is a further development of the 'accommodation' model, which allows one to say that not only the *cultural thought-forms* of the Old Testament, but the *ideas affirmed in it*, must be criticised and may be rejected. On this view we simply have to say that some actions, attitudes and assumptions in the Bible are not to be commended, that the theology of the Bible is not perfect, and that we are right to pass judgement on some aspects of it, in the New as well as the Old Testaments. At the Reformation, Martin Luther believed that the Gospel of grace which he had discovered in his own experience offered a standard by which to judge the Scriptures – those parts of Scripture which preached 'Law' rather than 'Gospel' were of less value than those in which the Gospel shone clearly (and there were some books in the New Testament as well as the Old which needed criticism on these grounds).

James Barr has argued in detail for a theological critique of the Scriptures in a large number of publications. The following passage from one of his earlier works illustrates his case, with reference to the kind of text which we are thinking about here:

> The popular 'progressive' arguments against the Old Testament, which commonly cite the moral shockingness of the destruction of the Canaanites, or the unforgiving ethos of the imprecatory Psalms, make sense only on the assumption of a quite fundamentalistic directness of interpretation and application. These arguments make sense only if it is assumed that the reading of something in the Bible can only be a token of universal approbation, so that modern Christians are being invited to delight directly in the killing of ancient Canaanites or to regard the dropping of babies from city walls as an inherently desirable action. No one today however seriously holds these assumptions. Moral judgements by the modern reader are entirely proper, but can only be usefully made when he has examined the background for such stories or poems, the sociology of the period, the question whether the stories are historically true, the reasons why they are told in this form, and the theological arguments within the Israelite tradition which they are used to sustain. (Barr, 1972, p. 165)

EXERCISE
📖 **Read Psalm 137.**

This is one of the so-called 'imprecatory psalms' – psalms which invoke destruction and suffering on the Psalmist's enemies. Do Barr's points in the previous extract help to understand how such a psalm could be part of Christian Scripture?

Religious language

It could be argued that no language – not even the language of the Bible – gives us a direct access to an exact picture of God. All talk about God is metaphor: it uses images such as that of 'father' which are both like God (he cares for his creation) but also unlike God (he does not beget children). The key point for us is to discern which metaphors are central or controlling, and which are merely subsidiary.

T E Fretheim has argued that all metaphorical language about God has both a 'yes' (elements which illumine our understanding of God) and a 'no' (elements which, if pressed, would obscure our understanding of God). When we are reading the Old Testament, therefore, we have to exercise some discernment about which metaphors have more of the 'yes' element, and which more of the 'no'.

> Not all metaphors have the same value; they have varying degrees of revelatory capacity. For example, Hosea's image of God as parent (11:1) has more value than does his image of God as dry rot (5:12). Some metaphors bespeak so much no that they obscure who God is (e.g., God is a killer of children); others are used so often that they may throw the image of God out of balance (e.g., father) . . . But all metaphors, whether of high value or low, are only partial visions of the truth about God; *no* metaphor is fully correspondent to the actual God. (Fretheim and Froelich, 1998, pp. 118–119)

On this view, then, our puzzlement over the difficult texts of the Old Testament (and the New, for that matter) comes from our failure to recognise that within the limits of our language we can only say 'God is something like this'. We are not committed to claiming that Psalm 137 or Joshua 10 are exact depictions of actions of which God approves. The difficulty with this approach is that it assumes that we have some solid ground of judgement from which we can discern which are the enlightening metaphors and which the obscuring ones.

Sola scriptura

An interpreter might take quite a different line and argue that difficult passages in the Old Testament are just as revelatory as more congenial passages. It might be said that it is only our preconceptions which make us shy away from the tough images of the Old Testament, and that these are, after all, no harsher than some of the things we find in the New Testament. The 'accommodation' and (still more) the 'theological critique' approaches assume that we can and should bring a standard of criticism to bear on the Scriptures as we read them. So, in this instance, we might assume that commands to massacre people tell us something about the culture of ancient Israel, but little or nothing about the nature of the God we worship.

The Reformation watchword of *sola scriptura* meant 'by Scripture alone', and expressed a Protestant conviction that Scripture is not to be judged by any external rule, including our convictions about what is morally proper. The following passage is from a writer who believes that the tough passages like Joshua 10 tell us as much about God as any other part of the Bible. The writer makes a case for seeing Joshua 10 as speaking of the Christian God – but how convincing is his case?

> As awkward as it may appear, one cannot abstract the slaughter of the Canaanite tribes from the larger question of the wrath of God, of God's response to multiplying sin. If one excises large swaths of the Pentateuch and of Joshua, should one then excise all that Jesus says about hell, much of the Apocalypse, and so forth? Our first duty, surely, is to listen, and try to understand . . . God's wrath, including that displayed in the extermination of Canaanite tribes is tied . . . to the entire biblical plot-line. It is of a piece with the flood, the Exile, the destruction of Jerusalem, and of hell itself; conversely, it is tied, as the dark side, the side of sin and hate and war and destruction, to the story of our redemption, stemming from the love of God intervening on our behalf, when he had no obligation to do so. (Carson, 1996, p. 237)

EXERCISE

The five ways of appropriating the Old Testament as Christian Scripture could be categorised variously:

- the 'accommodation' and the 'sola scriptura' views attempt to defend the ideas affirmed in the text as Christian ideas, while the 'development', 'religious language' and 'theological critique' views make it possible to reject some aspects as incompatible with the Christian Gospel;
- the 'development', 'accommodation', 'religious language' and 'theological critique' views all begin with the assumption that there is a standard by which we may judge the text as acceptable or not – the 'sola scriptura' view rejects this assumption.

Do you find any of these approaches more helpful than others in making sense of the Old Testament as Christian Scripture?

Further reading

Achtemeier, E (1995), The canon as the voice of the living God, in C E Braaten and R W Jenson (eds), *Reclaiming the Bible for the Church*, pp. 119–130, Edinburgh, T and T Clark.

Baker, D L (1976), *Two Testaments, One Bible*, Leicester, IVP.

Barr, J (1972), *The Bible in the Modern World*, London, SCM.

Barr, J (1982), *Old and New in Interpretation*, London, SCM (second edition).

Barton, J (1984), *Reading the Old Testament: method in biblical study*, London, Darton, Longman and Todd.

Barton, J (1997), *What is the Bible?* London, SPCK (second edition).

Carson, D A (1996), *The Gagging of God: Christianity confronts pluralism*, Leicester, Apollos.

Fretheim, T E and Froelich, K (1998), *The Bible as Word of God in a Postmodern Age*, Minneapolis, Fortress.

Goldingay, J (1990), *Approaches to Old Testament Interpretation*, Leicester, IVP (second edition).

Goldingay, J (1995), *Models for Interpretation of Scripture*, Grand Rapids, Michigan, Eerdmans and Carlisle, Paternoster.

9. WORDS AND THE WORD: THE TEXT OF SCRIPTURE

Introduction

We live in a world largely shaped by the printed word. The biblical writers and their readers lived in a world of manuscripts. It is difficult for us to appreciate just what a gap lies between our attitude to the written word and theirs, or what a difference printing has made to the status and use of the written word. We recognise, of course, that from the time that movable type began to be used in Europe in the fifteenth century, texts could be copied more cheaply than had ever been possible before. But printing also made possible a new *standardisation* of the text.

Until Gutenberg published his printed Latin Bible in 1455/6, every Bible and every portion of the Bible had been reproduced by hand as a manuscript. Manuscripts are individual productions, and each one contains features which mark it out from every other manuscript. Most contain differences of wording, largely due to the problems of copying text accurately. Our printed Bibles of today are, by way of contrast, so identical that every page of a particular edition will contain exactly the same words. We can guide people to follow a particular passage in church, for instance, by giving them a page number. This would have been impossible for most of the Bible's history, not only because manuscript versions were costly to produce, but because every manuscript was slightly different.

Reflecting on experience
Have you ever tried to copy any extensive amount of text by hand?
- Did you make any mistakes?
- What problems does copying entail (such as returning to the right place each time)?

As an experiment, you might try copying out the opening two paragraphs of this chapter, noting your difficulties and mistakes.

Manuscript adventures

Printing, of course, does not guarantee accuracy. Setting and proofreading a printed text can be done sloppily and can result in errors entering the printed text. There are plenty of examples of this happening in the history of Bible production (see Metzger, in Metzger and Coogan, 1993, pp. 143–144). Perhaps the most notorious was the 'Adulterous Bible' of 1631, in which the word 'not' was left out of Exodus 20:14, giving the reading: 'Thou shalt commit adultery'!

Conversely, manuscripts can be copied accurately, given care and time. The Hebrew text of the Old Testament has been transmitted remarkably faithfully, at least since the early Middle Ages. However, even with the Hebrew Old Testament, variations have occurred (see Tov, 1992).

In this chapter we will concentrate on the New Testament. The problems of the Old Testament text are different in detail and would require a great deal more discussion to set them in context, but the texts of the Old and New Testaments raise the same essential issues for our understanding of the nature of the Bible.

On the whole it is likely, even taking into account the points conceded in the previous three paragraphs (printing can introduce errors and hand copying can be done accurately), that texts copied by hand will contain more variations than texts which have been printed. Given the tendency for variations to creep into manuscripts when they are copied, it is not surprising that in the case of the New Testament thousands upon thousands of variations of wording exist in the manuscripts which have come down to us.

None of this would be of much concern to the reader of the Bible if we possessed the original copies (autographs) of all of the books of the Bible, in the state in which their authors wrote them. As it is, though, we possess no autographs of any biblical book. All we have are manuscript copies, some written near the time of composition but most a long time afterwards. Some have been copied with care, and are based on copies which themselves had been carefully made, while others are relatively careless. But without the originals against which to check them, how can we tell which are the reliable ones and which are the unreliable? Or, if we decide that we can identify the work of careful copyists, how can we be sure at any particular point that an otherwise scrupulous craftsman has not made an uncharacteristic mistake, or that he has not taken it into his head to make an intentional 'improvement' of his text? Or what if a conscientious copyist has accurately reproduced a text which one of his less careful predecessors in the chain of copying had already corrupted?

Textual criticism

These are the problems addressed by 'textual criticism', which is the branch of biblical study devoted to examining the wording of the manuscripts of the Old and New Testaments, working out how the various differences between them have arisen and what is most likely to represent the original text. There are a number of useful books and articles intended to introduce and explain this branch of study with its numerous and fascinating problems (Metzger, 1968; Aland and Aland, 1987; Vaganay, 1991; Patzia, 1995).

Our purpose here is not to go over ground which is covered elsewhere, but to ask what this textual variation *means* for our understanding of the Bible.

It could be argued that the significance of the variants, many though they are, is not serious: 'If the variant readings are so numerous, it is because the witnesses are so numerous. But all the witnesses, and all the types which they represent, agree on every article of Christian belief and practice' (Bruce, 1971, p. 189).

It could, though, be argued that the nature of this textual variation should make us reconsider what we think the Bible is. One recent writer on the subject, after noting very carefully the extent of textual variation in some key areas of the New Testament, concluded that we should think of the second century as a time when the form of the text was 'free', that is, uncontrolled by ecclesiastical authority and open to alteration by scribes. He suggests that we cannot ever be completely sure that we have recovered the original wording of the New Testament. Indeed, we notice that the scribes of the early period passed on the text in a very free manner, so we should remain content with a New Testament whose original text is probably irrecoverable. Why should we imagine that we need a 'solid' original text in any case?

> Expressed most starkly, the issue is whether the attempt to recover a single original text is consonant with the character of the free-

manuscript tradition, or whether it is driven by external demands: in particular, those of churches for authoritative texts ... and of scholars for a sure foundation on which to build their theories ... Our analysis of the material can leave no doubt in the matter. (Parker, 1997, p. 209)

A textual problem: the 'bloody sweat' passage

📖 **Read Luke 22:43–44.** Many textual problems are a matter merely of word order or the omission or addition of a single word, but the problem of Luke 22:43–44 is more substantial. It concerns a passage containing an entire narrative scene from the passion of Christ, the story of the 'bloody sweat'. Did Luke write these words or were they added by a copyist at a later stage?

In several early manuscripts this passage does not appear at all. In others, it appears with some kind of mark against it, indicating that the scribes had their doubts about its authenticity (rather like modern translations which alert readers to the fact that 'other ancient authorities omit verses 43 and 44'). In a few manuscripts it appears in a different place (after Matthew 26:39). In some, it appears here without any indication of doubt.

Scholars who think this story was *not* originally part of Luke's text point to this textual uncertainty. They argue that this was a piece of oral tradition which Luke did not include in his gospel. The fact that some scribes placed it here, while others put it in Matthew, is highly significant: it is the tell-tale sign that it did not originally belong in either place, but that different scribes, knowing the story and recognising its interest, decided independently of one another to add it to the gospels, some scribes (or one?) in Luke and some (or one?) in Matthew. It is (on this view) rather like the story of the woman caught in adultery (conventionally placed as John 7:53 to 8:11, but slotted into other places by other manuscripts – including several which place it in Luke's gospel – and omitted entirely by several manuscripts).

Scholars who think that Luke did indeed write this passage argue that in the second century Christians would have disapproved on theological grounds of stories which made Jesus seem too vulnerable, weak and human. This 'bloody sweat' passage would have offended them, so they probably removed it, and this explains why it had dropped out of many manuscripts.

The simple fact is that nobody can tell us with certainty whether or not this passage was written by Luke. It is a matter of weighing arguments and forming a judgement on the balance of probability.

EXERCISE

Do you think it is necessary to defend a passage such as Luke 22:43–44, which has fed Christian devotion down the ages? Or should we be willing to cut it out of our Bibles if we conclude that it was not part of Luke's work?

To think the issues of this question through, you might consider some of the further questions which it throws up.

- Would the 'bloody sweat' story have less value if it proved to be a piece of early oral tradition which did not happen to get into Luke's original text?
- If it was a piece of early oral tradition, does it matter whether it was Luke or some unknown copyist who found a home for it at this point in the story? Does Luke's adoption of this orphan story give it an authority, *or* as an early piece of tradition, does it have an inherent authority and interest?
- Does the fact that it has been 'Scripture' for millions of Christian readers over many centuries make it Scripture, even if Luke did not write it?

The manuscript foundations of the New Testament

A printed New Testament looks very secure and solid. When we open it and read, say, Luke's gospel, we expect to find that we are reading Luke's very words. It is something of a surprise to learn that the text we are reading is the result of thousands of decisions comparable to the one which we have just thought about in connection with Luke 22:43–44.

We must put this observation in perspective. F F Bruce's comment above, to the effect that no textual variant calls any doctrine of Christianity into question, is fully justified. Huge numbers of the textual variants concern only such matters as word order or spelling, which could not be reproduced in translation anyway. Very few variants are as intrinsically significant as the 'bloody sweat' passage, or as the story of the woman taken in adultery. So we should not imagine that our manuscripts contain anything which directly calls Christian faith into question. They do not. But they do make us think about the nature of Scripture.

The printed New Testament is a house built on the foundations of manuscripts. We do not normally notice or think about the foundations of a house, and they are invisible except to those who dig down to inspect them. Rather similarly the manuscript 'foundations' of our New Testament are not normally visible to most readers. We assume that the foundations, whether of a house or of our New Testament, are sound and solid. How justified are we in making this assumption in the case of the New Testament? Our inspection of one small part of the foundations (Luke 22:43–44) showed us that it is worth knowing something more of this hidden part of the New Testament if we are to understand better the more visible and obvious part, the modern printed text.

A textual problem: did Paul compromise in Jerusalem?

📖 **Read Galatians 2:3–5.** Here Paul explains how he stood firm when pressed to make a concession to 'false believers' by obliging his Gentile colleague Titus to be circumcised during a rather highly-charged visit to Jerusalem (possibly, though not certainly, the visit decribed in Acts 15:1–29). He would not compromise, even for a moment (v. 5).

Or did he stand firm? Some manuscripts omit two Greek words (or their equivalents in the case of Latin translations) meaning 'to whom we did not', at the start of verse 5. The sense of the verse would then be 'We *did* submit to them for a moment, so that the truth of the Gospel might always remain with you.' These manuscripts therefore give a different picture: not Paul resisting pressure but Paul behaving flexibly, 'as a Jew, in order to win Jews' (1 Corinthians 9:20).

There are two things to take into consideration in deciding which reading is likely to be correct. The first consideration is the manuscript evidence. The evidence for the second reading ('we did submit') is rather thin. Only one Greek manuscript has this reading and all the other evidence comes from Latin, not Greek, sources.

The second consideration is intrinsic probability. Is it likely that Paul would have stood firm or would he have conceded on this point? How would compromising on such a key issue have ensured for his Galatian converts 'that the truth of the Gospel might always remain with you' (v. 5b)?

EXERCISE

Do you think Paul allowed Titus to be circumcised? Or did he refuse to let this happen? Which text is right?

Papyri, the earliest survivors

The early Christians made many copies of their Scriptures but few have survived. Partly this is because they wrote on papyrus, a material rather like modern paper, made from the papyrus reed rather than from wood or rag pulp. Though quite tough and durable, papyrus does eventually rot, but a wonderful chance has preserved large numbers of papyrus documents on ancient rubbish heaps in Egypt, where the arid climate has allowed them to survive. Since the late nineteenth century, thousands of such documents have been found, and over a hundred portions of the New Testament have now been identified among them. A document written on papyrus is usually called simply 'a papyrus' for short, and the plural is 'papyri'. Scholars treasure these early papyri, but we must not forget that they come from a restricted area of rural Egypt: the vast majority of papyri have perished.

The earliest New Testament manuscript to have survived is a small portion of John (18:31–33 and 37–38), preserved on a scrap of papyrus less than three inches by four, and now in the John Rylands Library at Manchester. It can only be dated from the style of handwriting which its scribe used, but this puts it, by general agreement, in the first half of the second century and a date as early as AD 125 is often suggested. Survivals become more frequent from about AD 200, and include some manuscripts with quite substantial portions of several books.

No other books from the ancient world have survived in such early copies, or in such a quantity of examples. But we need to bear in mind that these papyri were being copied apparently without supervision or control. There was no central authority to impose a standard form of words on the copyists of this early period (first to third centuries). So, the fact that many papyri are old does not necessarily mean that they always give us the most reliable form of the New Testament text.

Uncials, the legacy of respectability

From the fourth century onwards a new type of biblical manuscript appeared. Whereas the papyri were written on a cheap material, in the characteristic writing of everyday communication, and have only been recovered from rubbish heaps, these new manuscripts were written on expensive vellum or parchment, in beautiful calligraphy, and numbers of them have been preserved by Churches and libraries through the centuries to the present day.

This type of manuscript is often known as 'uncial', after the style of writing used by their scribes. Uncial writing is clear and regular. Producing these manuscripts must have been a slow, and therefore expensive, business which called for the skills of trained scribes, to say nothing of the cost and professional skill required to produce the vellum on which the scribes wrote.

The production of these uncial manuscripts seems to have been made possible by the accession to power of the Emperor Constantine (AD 312), who favoured Christianity. Under his patronage, and that of his Christian successors, the Church became respectable and wealthy. From this point it had the financial support necessary to produce these beautiful and expensive manuscripts.

Nearly three hundred uncial manuscripts exist, and they include some of the most valuable witnesses to the New Testament text. Among them are:

- the Codex Vaticanus – a fourth-century manuscript of the whole Bible (though part of the New Testament is lost), now in the Vatican Library in Rome;
- the Codex Sinaiticus – another fourth-century manuscript of the whole Bible (and the only uncial to contain the entire New Testament without any sections missing), Sinaiticus was discovered in the monastery of St Catherine on Mount Sinai in 1844 and was purchased for the British Museum in 1933;
- the Codex Alexandrinus, probably fifth century, which was presented to King Charles I by the Patriarch of Jerusalem and is now displayed in the British Museum along with Sinaiticus.

The period of the uncials seems to have also been a time of attempts to standardise the wording of the New Testament. It was possible to regulate copying in the great ecclesiastical centres which produced these manuscripts to a greater degree than had been possible during the preceding centuries.

Eventually a form of wording emerged as standard, and from the fifth century onwards most Greek manuscripts have a much more regular and predictable text. Scholars call this regular form of words the 'Byzantine' text, since it was established as the standard for the Churches of the Byzantine Empire. Variations still arose, of course, as scribes still made occasional slips or came across alternative readings which they might add to their text. But Greek manuscripts written after the fifth century tend to show less variety in wording than the earlier manuscripts. Two influences are likely to have contributed to this textual constancy: an increasing respect for the exact wording of the New Testament as Scripture, and tighter ecclesiastical supervision of the copying process.

Windows onto the text: the versions and the Fathers

We have two other windows onto the wording of early copies of the New Testament: citations of the New Testament by the Church Fathers, and the early translations of the New Testament into languages other than Greek.

When Fathers of the Church quote from the books of the New Testament, they often give us evidence of the particular wording of manuscripts of the New Testament known to them. This evidence can give valuable clues to the contents of these (now lost) manuscripts.

The early Christians were very keen to read their Scriptures in their own languages, so translations were made in the first few centuries of the New Testament out of Greek into Latin, Syriac (the language of Syria), the languages of Egypt and the languages of several other areas in which Christianity had taken a hold (Metzger, 1977). These versions (as they are known) also give a valuable indication of the form of Greek words underlying their translation.

A textual problem: how does the Lord's Prayer end?

We all know that the Lord's Prayer ends: 'For yours is the kingdom, the power and the glory, for ever and ever, Amen.' But if we read the Lord's Prayer in a modern translation, we may be surprised at what we find.

EXERCISE
📖 **Read Matthew 6:13.**

Is this the ending you expect? Why do you think that most modern translations leave out the familiar ending?

The familiar ending is omitted because a large part of our textual witnesses do not have these words in them. These include two of the major uncials mentioned above, Sinaiticus and Vaticanus. Many early Latin manuscripts and translations into Egyptian languages do not have it, and neither does Origen when he quotes the Lord's Prayer.

The familiar ending is first found in a manual of Church order called the *Didache*, or *Teaching of the Apostles*, which probably dates from the early second century. It later appears in numerous Greek manuscripts, as well as in translations (in various forms).

EXERCISE

What has happened here? Either the familiar ending was present in the gospel as Matthew wrote it, or it has been added afterwards. Here are some questions to consider in coming to a decision about this:

- Is it more likely that a copyist would remove the words or that he would add them? What reasons might he have for either action?
- Read 1 Chronicles 29:11–13. Is it possible, or even likely, that at some point in the Church's use of the Lord's Prayer, an ending has been added to the prayer to make it more suitable for liturgical use (the *Didache* indicates use by the Church), and that this ending has been modelled on 1 Chronicles?
- A further question to think over: if modern textual critics are right, and the familiar ending was no part of the original prayer, should it be removed? Should we 'purify' the Lord's Prayer – or is it legitimate to do what the *Didache* had already done and adapt it for use in liturgy?

The text and the nature of Scripture

This chapter has looked at the foundations of the New Testament before the advent of printing gave the wording of the text a fixed form. We have noted how we know about the state of these foundations through the study of manuscripts, from quotations in the Fathers, and from the evidence of the early translations.

This chapter has also shown that inspection of the foundations reveals some unexpected things about the wording of the New Testament. A totally controlled and regular pattern of words could only exist after printing was invented, but the example of Jewish scribes who copy the Torah meticulously shows that, given the will, a large measure of standardisation can be achieved in manuscript copying. However, no real effort seems to have been made to exercise any control over Christian copyists of the New Testament until the fourth century. From the first to the fourth centuries copying was uncontrolled (as far as we may see), and many scholars believe that copyists in the earliest period (second century) also allowed themselves the greatest freedom in altering their texts. What does this imply about their attitude to the New Testament as Scripture?

We might have expected a fairly uniform wording to have gradually diversified in the process of copying. But in fact the opposite appears to be the case: the oldest manuscripts and the earliest quotations in the Fathers show the greatest diversity, while the process of imposing unity on the text came later. We have a pattern of initial diversity being superseded by the relative uniformity of the Byzantine text.

The extent of this diversity should not be overdrawn: the overall sense of each New Testament book is not radically altered by textual variation, even though particular points of detail are affected (as we saw when looking at Luke 22:43–44 and Galatians 2:3–5). No doubt the true original text is preserved somewhere among the variants we have – although some textual critics do entertain the possibility that at some points *all* our manuscripts may be wrong. But how do we know which is exactly the right wording? Does it matter that we may not be able to say with total confidence *exactly* what Luke or Paul, or any other New Testament writer, originally wrote?

EXERCISE

Look again at the quotation from Parker towards the start of this chapter. Do we need to know the exact original wording of the New Testament? Why do we need to know this – or, if you conclude the opposite, how can we manage with a New Testament whose exact original wording cannot be determined?

Further reading

Aland, A and Aland, B (1987), *The Text of the New Testament*, Leiden, Brill and Grand Rapids, Michigan, Eerdmans.

Bruce, F F (1971), *The Books and the Parchments*, London, Pickering and Inglis (third edition).

Metzger, B (1968), *The Text of the New Testament: its transmission, corruption and restoration*, Oxford, Oxford University Press.

Metzger, B (1977), *The Early Versions of the New Testament: their origins, transmission and limitations*, Oxford, Oxford University Press.

Parker, D C (1997), *The Living Text of the Gospels*, Cambridge, Cambridge University Press.

Patzia, A G (1995), *The Making of the New Testament: origin, collection, canon*, Downers Grove, Illinois, InterVarsity and Leicester, Apollos.

Tov, E (1992), *Textual Criticism of the Hebrew Bible*, Minneapolis, Fortress.

Vaganay, L (1991), *An Introduction to New Testament Textual Criticism*, Cambridge, Cambridge University Press.

10. BIBLICAL AUTHORITY TODAY

Introduction

This chapter draws together much of what has been discussed and thought over in the preceding parts of this book. We can only clarify what we think the authority of the Bible is once we have an idea of what the Bible itself is. In thinking about the Bible's authority, we have to bear in mind what we may have concluded about inspiration and the qualities or properties of the Bible as Scripture, we have to consider how the Bible relates to science and to history, and we have to recall what we have discovered about the formation of the Scriptures (canon) and the transmission of the text.

Reflecting on experience
As a way of bringing your ideas into focus, it will help to turn to p. 104 and try to respond again to the statements you looked at in Chapter 1.

Compare the answers you give now with those you gave at the start. Have they changed at all? If so, can you say how and why? If not, do you consider you may have different *reasons* for believing what you do believe?

Defining biblical authority

Most Christians would probably say that they believe the Bible has an important part to play in Christian life and is significant for the Church. Many would express that importance in terms of 'authority'. But what do we mean by 'authority'?

	Agree strongly	Agree	Neither agree nor disagree	Disagree	Disagree strongly
1. The Bible is inspired by God	AS	A	N	D	DS
2. God speaks to people through the words of the Bible	AS	A	N	D	DS
3. Modern scholars have weakened people's confidence in the Bible	AS	A	N	D	DS
4. There are no errors in the Bible	AS	A	N	D	DS
5. Science makes the Bible hard to accept	AS	A	N	D	DS
6. The Old Testament sometimes contradicts the New	AS	A	N	D	DS
7. Readings from the Apocrypha should not be included in Christian worship	AS	A	N	D	DS
8. Christians ought to believe what the Bible says	AS	A	N	D	DS

The Bible's authority is its power to shape Christian faith and practice. It has, by general agreement, a form of normative authority for Christians: that is, it functions as a standard to which appeal can be made. Christians will appeal to the Bible to determine what they should believe and do in a sense in which they would not appeal to any other document. Christians will rely on the Bible to feed and nourish their spiritual life in a way in which they will rely on no other book.

However, Christians do turn to other sources to form their ideas of what they should believe and do. In Chapter 8 we considered the problems posed by passages such as Joshua 10 and Psalm 137. Most Christians find that the violence embraced by those passages is something they want to criticise. Where do we find a criterion by which to criticise the Scripture, if the Scripture is the authority for Christian faith?

In Chapters 6 and 7 we looked at the formation of the canon and found that the Bible did not drop complete from heaven – as one writer has put it, 'some with maps at the end and some without'. The Christian Scriptures were assembled over a period of centuries. Decisions were made (though we are not well informed about them) as to which books were in and which were out of this collection of Scripture. Disagreements persist on these issues. Why does *this* collection of books have authority for Christians, and not other collections, some of which may be equally ancient?

Biblical authority in a modern context

The idea of the Bible's authority has faced a number of challenges in the past few centuries. Or, to put it positively, a series of questions have obliged Christians to define their concept of biblical authority in a way which makes it credible to their contemporaries. We can identify three successive challenges in particular.

The Reformation: Scripture and tradition
The Reformation drew attention to the relationship of Scripture and Christian tradition. The Church recognised from at least the third century that it believed and did certain things because they were part of a *tradition* which had grown up, rather than because they were directly mandated by Scripture (worship on a Sunday is a conspicuous example). Until the Reformation it was generally assumed that the Church's tradition and Scripture coincided. The Reformers, though, believed that much Church tradition had gone astray, and had to be reformed in the light of Scripture. Scripture, for them, had an authority which set it above the teaching and tradition of the Church. In response, the Roman Catholic Church maintained that because the Holy Spirit keeps the Church faithful to the teaching of the Scripture, the authentic teaching

office of the Church (*magisterium*) will always reliably teach the truth. The Council of Trent established what has been called a 'supplementary' or 'two-source' theory of authority (Scripture *and* tradition), while the Reformers developed an 'ancillary' theory (tradition *under* Scripture) (Bauckham, 1988, pp. 118–125).

The Enlightenment and after: Scripture and reason

The Enlightenment in the eighteenth century raised the problem of relating the Bible and reason. Under this heading we can consider two challenges to biblical authority.

First, the Enlightenment itself questioned *all* reliance on authority to establish the truth of a matter. Truths, of religion as of science, history or anything else, were to be found by the use of human reason. Immanuel Kant, probably the most influential of eighteenth-century philosophers, summed up the Enlightenment's message in this respect as: *sapere aude* – 'Dare to know' or 'Do not be afraid to think for yourself.' The claim that the Bible held an authority because it represented a divine revelation had to be subjected to criticism. Thinkers of the Enlightenment criticised what they found in the Bible if it appeared to conflict with conclusions reached on rational grounds (McGrath, 1998, pp. 221–226).

Second, the Enlightenment opened the way to the kind of biblical criticism whose impact we considered in Chapter 2, and to the questioning from science and history which were the subjects of Chapters 4 and 5. As a result, it became more difficult to regard the Bible as a series of oracles which had been given directly from God. The biblical books appeared to be products of their time and their culture. How could such human books have a divine authority? Instead of God's word to humanity, were they (merely) human words about God?

The postmodernist challenge: authority and manipulation

In the final quarter of the twentieth century, postmodernist thinkers reacted against what they saw as the absolutist tendencies of the Enlightenment tradition. The Enlightenment, and the 'modernist' cast of thought which it engendered, assumed that there was *a* truth to be grasped – a single, universally valid way of grasping reality. Postmodernists deny this. In the postmodernist view, all 'truth' is merely a way of seeing things which has been created by particular individuals or groups.

Postmodernists reject what they describe as 'metanarratives' – that is, total world-views which provide a framework for all understanding of reality. Such metanarratives are inevitably part of an attempt by one group to impose control on others and subdue alternative 'truths'. Authority is necessarily authoritarian. We have seen one example of this kind of argument in P R Davies' interpretation of Old Testament canon-formation as an exercise in power and control (Chapter 6). Postmodernism therefore goes beyond the Enlightenment critique of authority by rejecting the notion of 'authority' altogether. In the postmodernist view there can be no authoritative voice defining what all should believe or do – and we should be suspicious of the concealed motives of power and manipulation behind any claim to have found such a voice (McGrath, 1998, pp. 243–245; Bauckham, 1999).

EXERCISE

What do you see as the greatest challenge to the idea of the Bible as 'authority' today? Do you think that you see the problem in the same way as other people you know? Do people outside the Christian faith community see this issue in the same terms as those within that community?

A biblical authority for today

So far in this chapter we have seen something of the context in which a contemporary understanding of biblical authority has to be framed. We have also been reminded of what previous chapters have shown us of the challenges and difficulties attendant on the idea of an authoritative Scripture. We will now look at some of the possible responses to all of this.

Authority or resource?

A strong current in British theology in particular has argued that the Bible should not be regarded as an authority, informing Christians what to believe and guiding them in what to do. Rather, it should be seen as a resource, as something to be drawn upon to help belief and action, but, by implication, something which need *not* be drawn upon when it does not help. Among those advocating this kind of understanding would be two theologians whose work we have already encountered,

James Barr and John Barton, together with several other well-known thinkers such as Maurice Wiles and John Hick.

This current of thought has little difficulty in accommodating any of the critical issues which we have encountered in this book. It does not make any special claim for the historical accuracy of the scriptural writings, or for their theological adequacy. It can accept the idea that the canon of Old and New Testaments was drawn up arbitrarily. However, to look at the Bible in this way raises the same kind of question which we considered when thinking about the Old Testament as Christian Scripture: on what basis can we say that some aspects of the Bible are a resource for which we have no use?

Authority is, in a definition proposed by the Roman Catholic theologian Avery Dulles, 'that which (or the person whom) one has reason to trust' (cited in Fretheim and Froelich, 1998, p. 14). Approaching the Bible merely as a resource might effectively be saying that the Bible is so compromised by our critical study of it that in certain respects we can *not* accord it our trust. We might suggest that this approach has at least one thing in common with that of Marcion: it assumes that there is a higher and better standard by which we can discern what is to be approved and what rejected in the Scriptures. The second-century Church refused to accept Marcion's kind of criticism partly because it believed that it could not pass this kind of judgement on the Scriptures.

EXERCISE

📖 **Read Jeremiah 20:7–12.**

This passage illustrates the difficulty, in Jeremiah's experience, of listening to God and of coping with a message from him. It expresses the prophet's indignation that God had 'enticed' or 'duped' him, leading him to say and do things which made him the object of derision.

If Jeremiah's message ran counter to what most people expected to hear from God (v. 7), could the same hold good of Scripture as a whole? If there are difficult things to accept, what do we do with those things?

The authority of the prototype

Elizabeth Schüssler-Fiorenza has drawn a distinction, when considering authoritative religious writings, between what she has called an 'archetype' and a 'prototype'. The archetype is a fixed norm, a given standard against which all future developments are judged. A prototype, by contrast, is an initial sketch or outline. It contains the essential ideas but it is open to development and change. In fact its very essence is to invite alteration and growth in the light of further thought and experience. The authority of the Bible, she has suggested, is more like a prototype than an archetype. Instead of controlling and dominating Christian development in a negative way, it invites and even expects Christians down the ages to take its initial impetus and make of it what they can and should, using their own creative insight and having regard for their very changed circumstances.

N T Wright has drawn a similar picture of the way in which biblical authority might work, using the analogy of a play. Suppose, Wright suggests, there is a Shakespeare play of which only four acts exist. Shakespeare evidently intended there to be a fifth act, but how to provide it? The best way would be to give the parts (already delineated in the existing text) to trained and sensitive actors, who could immerse themselves in the play and who would then work out a fifth act for themselves.

> As we saw, part of the initial task of the actors chosen to improvise the new final act will be to immerse themselves with full sympathy in the first four acts, but not so as merely to parrot what has already been said. They cannot go and look up the right answers. Nor can they simply imitate the kinds of things that their particular character did in the early acts. A good fifth act will show a proper final development, not merely a repetition, of what went before. Nevertheless, there will be a rightness, a fittingness, about certain actions and speeches, about certain final moves in the drama, which will in one sense be self-authenticating, and in another gain authentification from their coherence with, their making sense of, the 'authoritative' previous text. (Wright, 1992, p. 141)

R Bauckham has put forward a similar picture of the Bible as 'metanarrative' – 'it sketches in narrative form the meaning of all reality' (Bauckham, 1999, p. 10). A crucial point about this biblical metanarrative is its unfinished nature: 'We ourselves play our part in writing the current chapter of the story, and for that purpose the overall biblical metanarrative functions authoritatively by setting the direction of the plot for us to follow' (Bauckham, 1999, p. 11).

EXERCISE

How do you respond to Wright's analogy of the unfinished play? What do you see as the strong points of this view? Are there weaknesses: is it, for instance, the *text* which has authority, or the story behind the text? (This problem does not arise with an entirely fictional text such as a Shakespearean play.)

A new paradigm

Much attention has been given in modern scholarship to the diversity of Scripture. The critical reading of biblical books does not regard them as so many oracles which should all speak with one voice: prayer and prophecy, and law and story are very different forms of literature. Some recent thoughts on biblical authority have tried to take account of this diversity (Bartlett, 1983).

J Goldingay has proposed that trying to view all of Scripture in an undifferentiated way as an authoritative, inspired guide represents an old paradigm, one which is now discredited by all the critical questions which we have been considering. It is time, Goldingay suggests, to reconsider biblical authority in the light of Scripture's evident diversity. Some parts of Scripture (the Pentateuch is a clear example) do indeed function as 'authoritative canon', but other parts function in other ways: narratives as 'witnessing tradition', prophets as 'inspired word', and wisdom as 'experienced revelation'. Not all of Scripture, therefore, serves to warn or proscribe or teach doctrines. Much of it (and, in Goldingay's view, probably the most significant part) serves to tell a story. Other parts give a word from God to particular situations, while others again reflect on human experience in the light of God's presence in the world.

The notion of 'authority' was stretched to cover Scripture as a whole when the Church itself turned into an authoritarian institution during its first few centuries:

> When the church began to function more fundamentally as an institution, the thinking that undergirded Roman law and government came to influence it and the technical term 'authority' was used not only to describe one hitherto unlabeled function inherent in one

specific part of the scriptures but to describe the function of scripture as a whole. (Goldingay, 1994, p. 6)

Conclusion: authority, intrinsic or extrinsic?

A person or institution has extrinsic authority when they have a power to command, whether we see the point of the command or not. An officer in the armed forces, for instance, exercises this kind of authority. Intrinsic authority is the authority of an acknowledged expert, of someone whose advice or instruction we can see is sensible and wise.

Which sort of authority does the Bible have? An understanding of inspiration (Chapter 3) which places a high value on the 'God-breathed' quality of Scripture will tend to emphasise Scripture's *extrinsic* authority: because it represents the word of God, it is to be listened to and followed. Someone who approaches Scripture from a more critical point of view (as we have explored it in various chapters) will tend to regard Scripture's authority as *intrinsic*: it will often give sound and credible advice and give rise to helpful ideas, but when it does not commend itself then we are at liberty to set it aside.

It is probably true to say, as Bauckham does (Bauckham, 1999, p. 4), that for most Christians the Bible has an authority which is a mixture of extrinsic and intrinsic. Perhaps in personal experience one might begin by taking the Bible as largely an extrinsic authority and then find that experience confirms its authority to us, so that we recognise it more and more as an intrinsic authority. Perhaps, also, the Church has over-emphasised the extrinsic, commanding, arbitrary authority of Scripture as the word of God. It is also the case that virtually no reader of Scripture takes all its statements as straightforward, binding commands like the orders of a military officer. All Christian readers exercise some criticism of the militaristic passages of the Old Testament, for instance (see Chapter 8).

However, a Bible which is seen as possessing *merely* an intrinsic authority might seem rather unsatisfactory. Extrinsic authority is effective because of the source of the communication, because of who is speaking rather than principally what is being said. Intrinsic authority is effective because of the content of what is communicated: it is something which we can recognise as right and sensible, from whatever source it comes. Christians have traditionally believed that the stories the Bible tells, the poetry it contains, the commands it issues, demand attention because they are Scripture, and whether they are congenial or otherwise, whether they fit easily into our culture or not, even (we may say) whether we listen to them or not, they nonetheless speak with authority.

Our task must be to discover what the authority of Scripture means for us today, and how, knowing what we know about its human origins and transmission, we still hear it as a word from God.

EXERCISE

Are there any things which you believe and do simply because 'the Bible tells me so', and that you would not believe or do if the authority of Scripture did not compel you?

- If so, then why do you consider that the Bible has the authority to mould your life in this way?
- If not, then what authority does the Bible have for you?

How would you describe the authority of the Bible – as essentially extrinsic or largely intrinsic?

Further reading

Bartlett, D L (1983), *The Shape of Scriptural Authority*, Philadelphia, Fortress.

Bauckham, R (1988), Scripture in relation to tradition and reason, in R Bauckham and B Drewery (eds), *Scripture, Tradition and Reason: a study in the criteria of Christian doctrine. Essays in honour of Richard P C Hanson*, pp. 117–145, Edinburgh, T and T Clark.

Bauckham, R (1999), *Scripture and Authority Today*, Grove Biblical Series 12, Cambridge, Grove Books.

Fretheim, T E and Froelich, K (1998), *The Bible as Word of God in a Postmodern Age*, Minneapolis, Fortress.

Goldingay, J (1994), *Models for Scripture*, Grand Rapids, Michigan, Eerdmans and Carlisle, Paternoster.

McGrath, A E (1998), *Historical Theology: an introduction to the history of Christian thought*, Oxford, Blackwell.

Wright, N T (1992), *The New Testament and the People of God*, London, SPCK.

GLOSSARY AND BIOGRAPHY

allegory a way of presenting ideas so that each object or person stands for and represents another. For example, an allegorical interpretation of the parable of the Good Samaritan might claim that the Good Samaritan himself stands for Christ, the wounded man is fallen humanity, the innkeeper the Church, and so on.

Apocrypha a collection of Jewish literature contained in the Roman Catholic canon of the Old Testament, but not found in the Hebrew Bible and so relegated to an appendix to the Old Testament by the Reformers of the sixteenth century. Also called the *deuterocanonical books*.

Bultmann, Rudolf (1884–1976) one of the leading New Testament scholars of the twentieth century. Among his contributions to biblical interpretation was his argument that we must 'demythologise' the text, that is recognise that 'mythical' talk of apparently *objective* entities and events (angels, demons, miracles) is best understood as referring to *subjective* attitudes, feelings and decisions.

Calvin, John (1509–1564) French-born Protestant Reformer who aimed to produce a theology based upon the Bible as the word of God. His *Institutes of the Christian Religion* and his voluminous biblical commentaries had a great effect on subsequent Protestant understanding of the Bible.

creationism the name given to the view that the stories in Genesis 1 to 2 provide a valid *scientific* account of the origin of the world and the origins of life (that is creation by special interventions of God, species created separately and not through evolution, with a relatively brief time span for their existence, and so on).

Dead Sea Scrolls a collection of Jewish writings discovered in caves near the Dead Sea after 1947. They date from around the time of the New Testament and include the earliest Old Testament manuscripts known, together with commentaries and other writings. It is generally thought, though not proven, that they were produced by a religious community at nearby Qumran.

demythologising see **Bultmann, Rudolf**.

early Catholicism a term used by some scholars to characterise the increasingly institutionalised form of the Church at the end of the New Testament period. It is marked by more legalistic structures and a more sacramental view of both Church and ministry. The term often implies some criticism of this trend, seen as a decline from the spontaneous and charismatic phase of Christian life.

Enlightenment a movement of thought in the eighteenth century which claimed the right and necessity for individuals to discover truth on rational grounds, and not by appeal to authorities such as Scripture or the Church.

Fundamentalism a movement of thought particularly associated with American churches, which began in the early decades of the twentieth century and is marked by a belief that the Bible is inerrantly true in all that it affirms or teaches, whether in matters historical, scientific or religious.

inerrancy the doctrine that the Bible contains no errors, that is no statements of fact (including science, history and theological doctrine) that are not accurate.

infallibility the doctrine that the Bible does not fail in the purpose for which it is given. It is taken that the Bible's purpose is to nourish the people of God in their relationship with him, then it will (if it is infallible) unfailingly achieve that purpose.

inspiration the quality of being produced by a spirit. When applied to the Bible, inspiration affirms that the biblical text has been produced by the work of the Holy Spirit.

Lessing, Gotthold Ephraim (1729–1781) German playwright and critic of religion. Lessing applied the thought of the Enlightenment to the Bible, and questioned whether universal religious truths could depend on the accidental historical stories which the Bible tells.

Origen (c. 185–254) a Christian scholar and biblical interpreter from Alexandria in Egypt. His use of the allegorical method in the Christian study of the Bible was enormously influential on later biblical interpretation.

paradigm a model or structure for ordering ideas and concepts on a particular subject.

Pentateuch The first five books of the Old Testament (Genesis to Deuteronomy), known as the *Torah* in the Hebrew Bible and also traditionally known as the 'five Books of Moses'.

postmodernism a movement of thought which questions the validity of single, universally applicable systems of thinking, or universally valid meanings (in texts, for instance). Instead, it holds that meaning is created by particular communities or individuals, and that such meanings may not be acknowledged outside that community or by anyone other than the individual.

textual variant a passage of the Bible for which manuscript sources show differences of wording.

three-decker universe a way of describing the ancient conception of the earth as a flat surface, with heaven above the dome of the sky and the underworld (or hell) beneath the earth.

variant see **textual variant**.

Warfield, Benjamin B (1851–1921) American Protestant theologian whose work on the Bible laid the foundation for the modern 'inerrantist' view.

REFERENCES

Abraham,W J (1981), *The Divine Inspiration of Holy Scripture*, Oxford, Oxford University Press.

Achtemeier, E (1995), The canon as the voice of the living God, in C E Braaten and R W Jenson (eds), *Reclaiming the Bible for the Church*, pp. 119–130, Edinburgh, T and T Clark.

Achtemeier, P J (1980), *The Inspiration of Scripture: problems and proposals*, Philadelphia, Westminster.

Aland, A and Aland, B (1987), *The Text of the New Testament*, Leiden, Brill and Grand Rapids, Michigan, Eerdmans.

Astley, J (2000), *God's World*, London, Darton, Longman and Todd.

Baker, D L (1976), *Two Testaments, One Bible*, Leicester, IVP.

Barr, J (1972), *The Bible in the Modern World*, London, SCM.

Barr, J (1977), *Fundamentalism*, London, SCM.

Barr, J (1980), *Explorations in Theology 7*, London, SCM.

Barr J (1982), *Old and New in Interpretation*, London, SCM (second edition).

Barr, J (1983), *Holy Scripture: canon, authority, criticism*, Oxford, Clarendon.

Barr, J (1984), *Escaping from Fundamentalism*, London, SCM.

Barth, K (1975, ET second edition [Original German1932]), *Church Dogmatics 1: the doctrine of the word of God*, Vol. 1, Edinburgh, T and T Clark.

Bartlett, D L (1983), *The Shape of Scriptural Authority*, Philadelphia, Fortress.

Barton J (1984), *Reading the Old Testament: method in biblical study*, London, Darton, Longman and Todd.

Barton, J (1997a), *What is the Bible?*, London, SPCK (second edition).

Barton, J (1997b), *The Spirit and the Letter: studies in the biblical canon*, London, SPCK.

Bauckham, R (1988), Scripture in relation to tradition and reason, in R Bauckham and B Drewery (eds), *Scripture, Tradition and Reason: A study in the criteria of Christian doctrine. Essays in honour of Richard P C Hanson*, pp. 117–145, Edinburgh, T and T Clark.

Bauckham, R (1999), *Scripture and Authority Today*, Cambridge, Grove.

Beckwith, R T (1985), *The Old Testament Canon of the New Testament Church*, Grand Rapids, Michigan, Eerdmans.

Beckwith, R T (1993), Canon of the Hebrew Bible and the Old Testament, in B M

Metzger and M D Coogan (eds), *The Oxford Companion to the Bible*, pp. 100–102, Oxford, Oxford University Press.

Berkouwer, G C (1975), *Studies in Dogmatics: Holy Scripture*, ET Grand Rapids, Michigan, Eerdmans.

Blomberg, C (1997), *Jesus and the Gospels: an introduction and survey*, Leicester, Apollos.

Boice, J M (ed.) (1979), *The Foundation of Biblical Authority*, Glasgow, Pickering.

Boone, K C (1989), *The Bible Tells Them So: the discourse of Protestant fundamentalism*, London, SCM.

Brown, R E and Collins, R (1989), Canonicity, in R E Brown *et al.* (eds), *The New Jerome Biblical Commentary*, pp. 1034–1054, London, Geoffrey Chapman.

Bruce, F F (1971), *The Books and the Parchments*, London, Pickering and Inglis (third edition).

Bultmann, R (1984, originally published 1941), The New Testament and mythology: the problem of demythologizing the New Testament proclamation, in S M Ogden (ed.), *Rudolf Bultmann: New Testament and mythology and other basic writings*, pp. 1–43, London, SCM.

Burtchaell, J T (1969), *Catholic Theories of Biblical Inspiration since 1810: a review and critique*, Cambridge, Cambridge University Press.

Carson, D A (1996), *The Gagging of God: Christianity confronts pluralism*, Leicester, Apollos.

Chicago Statement on Biblical Inerrancy: on the internet at http://www.iclnet.org/pub/resources/text/history/chicago.stm.txt

Davies, P R (1998), *Scribes and Schools: The canonization of the Hebrew Scriptures*, London, SPCK.

Evans, C (1971), *Is 'Holy Scripture' Christian? and other questions*, London, SCM.

Evans, R (1999), *Using the Bible: studying the text*, London, Darton, Longman and Todd.

Fretheim, T E and Froelich, K (1998), *The Bible as Word of God in a Postmodern Age*, Minneapolis, Fortress.

Gibbon, E (1776/88), *The History of the Decline and Fall of the Roman Empire*, various editions.

Goldingay, J (1990), *Approaches to Old Testament Interpretation*, Leicester, IVP (second edition).

Goldingay, J (1994), *Models for Scripture*, Grand Rapids, Michigan, Eerdmans and Carlisle, Paternoster.

Goldingay, J (1995), *Models for Interpretation of Scripture*, Grand Rapids, Michigan, Eerdmans and Carlisle, Paternoster.

Kelsey, D H (1975), *The Uses of Scripture in Recent Theology*, London, SCM.

Küng, H (1994), *Infallible? an unresolved enquiry*, London, SCM.

McGrath, A E (ed.) (1995), *The Christian Theology Reader*, Oxford, Blackwell.

McGrath A (1998), *Historical Theology: an introduction to the history of Christian thought*, Oxford, Blackwell.

McMullin, E (1998), Galileo on science and Scripture, in P Machamer (ed.), *The Cambridge Companion to Galileo*, pp. 271–347, Cambridge, Cambridge University Press.

Marsden, G M (1980), *Fundamentalism and American Culture: the shaping of twentieth-century evangelicalism 1870–1925*, New York, Oxford University Press.

Marshall, I H (1982), *Biblical Inspiration*, London, Hodder and Stoughton.

Metzger, B (1968), *The Text of the New Testament: its transmission, corruption and restoration*, Oxford, Oxford University Press.

Metzger, B (1977), *The Early Versions of the New Testament: their origins, transmission and limitations*, Oxford, Oxford University Press.

Metzger, B M (1987), *The Canon of the New Testament*, Oxford, Oxford University Press.

Metzger, B M and Coogan, M D (eds) (1993), *The Oxford Companion to the Bible*, Oxford, Oxford University Press.

Newbigin, L (1986), *Foolishness to the Greeks*, London, SPCK.

O'Neill, J C (1991), *The Bible's Authority: a portrait gallery of thinkers from Lessing to Bultmann*, Edinburgh, T and T Clark.

Ord, D R and Coote, R B (1994), *Is the Bible True? understanding the Bible today*, London, SCM.

Packer, J I (1958), *'Fundamentalism' and the Word of God*, London, IVP.

Parker, D C (1997), *The Living Text of the Gospels*, Cambridge, Cambridge University Press.

Patzia, A G (1995), *The Making of the New Testament: origin, collection, canon*, Downers Grove, Illinois, InterVarsity and Leicester, Apollos.

Reventlow, H (1984), *The Authority of the Bible and the Rise of the Modern World*, London, SCM.

Rogerson, J (1984), *Old Testament Criticism in the Nineteenth Century: England and Germany*, London, SPCK.

Rogerson, J (1999), *An Introduction to the Bible*, London, Penguin.

Stanton, G (1997), *Gospel Truth? today's quest for Jesus of Nazareth*, London, HarperCollins (second edition).

Tov, E (1992), *Textual Criticism of the Hebrew Bible*, Minneapolis, Fortress.

Vaganay, L (1991), *An Introduction to New Testament Textual Criticism*, Cambridge, Cambridge University Press.

Vawter, B (1972), *Biblical Inspiration*, London, Hutchinson and Philadelphia, Westminster.

Warfield, B B (1948), *The Inspiration and Authority of the Bible*, Phillipsburg, New Jersey, Presbyterian and Reformed Publishing.

Westermann, C (1984), *Genesis 1–11*, London, SPCK.

Wright, N T (1992), *The New Testament and the People of God*, London, SPCK.

Yeago, D S (1997 [first published 1993]), The New Testament and the Nicene Dogma: a contribution to the recovery of theological exegesis, in S F Fowl (ed.), *The Theological Interpretation of Scripture: classic and contemporary readings*, pp. 87–100, Oxford, Blackwell.

ET indicates 'English translation'

INDEX OF THEMES

Applying for the Church Colleges' Certificate Programme

The certificate programme is available in Anglican Church Colleges of Higher Education throughout England and Wales. There are currently hundreds of students on this programme, many with no previous experience of study of this kind. There are no entry requirements. Some people choose to take Certificate courses for their own interest and personal growth, others take these courses as part of their training for ministry in the church. Some go on to complete the optional assignments and, after the successful completion of three courses, gain the Certificate. Courses available through the *Exploring Faith: theology for life* series are ideal for establishing ability and potential for studying theology and biblical studies at degree level, and they provide credit onto degree programmes.

For further details of the Church Colleges' Certificate programme, related to this series, please contact the person responsible for Adult Education in your local diocese or one of the colleges at the addresses provided:

The Administrator of Part-time Programmes, Department of Theology and Religious Studies, Chester College, Parkgate Road, CHESTER, CH1 4BJ ☎ 01244 375444

The Registry, Roehampton Institute, Froebel College, Roehampton Lane, LONDON, SW15 5PJ ☎ 020 8392 3087

The Registry, Canterbury Christ Church University College, North Holmes Road, CANTERBURY, CT1 1QU ☎ 01227 767700

The Registry, College of St Mark and St John, Derriford Road, PLYMOUTH, PL6 8BH ☎ 01752 636892

The Registry, Trinity College, CARMARTHEN, Carmarthenshire, SA31 3EP ☎ 01267 676767

Church Colleges' Programme, The Registry, King Alfred's College, Sparkford Road, WINCHESTER, SO22 4NR ☎ 01962 841515

Part-time Programmes, The Registry, College of St Martin, Bowerham Road, LANCASTER, LA1 3JD ☎ 01524 384529